CW00945242

Jane Mosley's
RECIPES

Designed and Published by Derbyshire Museum Service
1979

Acknowledgements

Frederick Soresby Ogden for the gift of Jane Mosley's manuscript, and access to his family papers and traditions

Janet Thornton for the preliminary transcription

Joan Sinar, Derbyshire County Archivist, for the final transcription, glossary and editorial matter

The Trustees of the National Portrait Gallery for permission to use the head of Princess Elizabeth

The Bodley Head for permission to use illustrations from Gerard's Herball

Glasgow University Library for the two centre page illustrations from Hannah Wolley's "The Queene-like Closet or Rich Cabinet" 1670

The Pilot Press for the illustration of cherry picking from "The Patchwork Book" 1943

Designed by Derbyshire Museum Service
Published in association with the Derbyshire Festival, 1979
Printed by Derwent Press Limited, Derby

DERBYSHIRE MUSEUM SERVICE, 1979
ISBN 0 906753 00 7

Contents

Warning Great care should be taken in identifying the wild plants mentioned in the recipes. Umbelliferous hedge plants such as Alexanders and Hedge Parsley should not be confused with other members of that family, notably Water Dropwort and Hemlock, which are extremely poisonous. Cultivated Water Cress should always be used as the wild variety may be unsafe for consumption, and can be confused with its toxic relatives.

Introduction

The Manuscript

Jane Mosley's book is a small octavo notebook bound in two thicknesses of coarse brown wrapping paper. It is written from one end to the middle opening with *to roast a neates tongue in the french fashion,* and from the other end also to the middle opening with *for the toothach.* The section opening with the recipe for the neat's tongue is penned very carefully to part way through the recipe for a white leach of almonds. The initial letters of the recipes in the section, though not of their titles, are frequently highly elaborate, and Jane has introduced two sub-headings: *Baked meats,* and *puddings* each ringed round. These recipes show every sign of very careful presentation and were probably written first in an early flush of enthusiasm, possibly as part of Jane's education for marriage and housekeeping. The remaining recipes in the section from *to stew beef* to *to Make a Caudle* are still neatly but far less carefully penned, and are not adorned with elaborate capitals. The recipes for the prevention of constipation, the pectoral infusion, gooseberry wine and raisin wine are in another less clerkly hand. The closing recipe for cherry wine is probably Jane Mosley's later hand. It is punctuated as she punctuates, and many of the letters are formed as she forms them. It is a smaller, more cursive script, less disciplined such as a woman might develop when freed from a copy book.

The second section opening with the recipe for *the tooth ach* is not written in so clerkly a style. So far from opening with elaborate initial letters the recipes, like their titles in both this and the first section, very seldom receive even a capital letter. Jane Mosley's name and a roundel divide the medical recipes from instructions on washing. In several of these instructions Jane uses a simple shorthand system which she continues through a set of recipes for sauces, but drops for the second set of medical recipes opening with her *excellent surfeit water.* The two recipes *for the worms* are in another hand which is probably not that contributing those for constipation etc in the first section. The closing recipes for the lead plaister, Sir Edward Terrills salve, mead and Princess Elizabeth's cake are in a larger version of the hand which closes the first section, and were probably also written by Jane Mosley in later life.

Jane Mosley's phraseology and that of her two friends or relatives who contributed some of the recipes is fairly standard late 17th or early 18th century usage. If the cook is to cover tightly she is advised to cover close. A dish is to be stirred *very tenderly for breaking the bread,* or in modern terms very gently lest the bread should be broken. The cook is instructed to take four eggs and take out two of the whites when four yolks but only two whites are to be used. Dishes are served to the table or in, presumably into the room where the family dined.

The spelling, which has been carefully reproduced, might seem strange today. The recipes were written before the days of dictionaries when words could properly be spelled in more than one way, and reflect the practice of the day. Jane Mosley's private trick of omitting the last letter y from words such as they, lay and day is confusing at first, but only holds up the reader for a moment. Where a word seems rather difficult to read the modern spelling or the missing letters have been supplied in square brackets. Most words which confuse the eye can be identified if read aloud.

So far as possible Jane Mosley's use of punctuation and capital letters has been preserved. She uses the comma and colon liberally, the semi-colon occasionally, and the full stop not at all. She does not open sentences with capital letters unless she is penning an elaborate decorative capital initial letter as she does at the beginning of many of the recipes in her first section. There are however breaks in the sense which are not marked by any punctuation. Between these breaks are recognisable sentences lacking only the initial capital and terminal full stop. These omissions have been supplied in this edition, and sentences transcribed in modern style. All other punctuation and use of capital letters follows the original except that an occasional comma has been added when it is omitted from an original list of ingredients.

Jane Mosley and her family

Jane Mosley was born probably in August 1669, for she was baptised on 2 September in that year. Her parents Gilbert Mosley or Moseley, junior, and Hester or Esther Mannering had married on 28 May, 1668, at St James', Duke Square, London. She was born into a family which had been in Brailsford for at least three generations, and her grandfather, Gilbert Mosley, senior, and his wife, Lucy, were still alive at her birth. Her parents probably lived with Gilbert and Lucy.

Gilbert Mosley, senior was the son of John Mosley of Brailsford by his second wife, Elizabeth. John leased a farm in Brailsford from Mr George Shirley of Stanton, Leicestershire. He died in 1609 leaving the remainder of the term of his lease to be shared equally between his wife during her widowhood and the eldest of his three sons by his first wife, Edward Mosley. His son Thomas was to have £5 when he finished his apprenticeship, and his son William £15 and a further £5 on marriage. Gilbert was to have such child's portion as his mother and Edward thought to give him. Each boy was left a silver spoon, and Elizabeth was left a spur royal and all the silver in her keeping *which is of king Edwards come*. This she was asked to divide with Gilbert who was probably a child when his father died. Though these sums sound small now they were in fact substantial legacies when a woman might be expected to live on 6d a week. John also left one shilling each to his sister, two brothers, and a nephew. His nephew at least also seems to have lived in Brailsford.

How long the family lived in Brailsford is not known because the parish registers are missing for the period before 1647. They may have descended from an early 16th century mercer named Mosley who lived in Ashbourne, but family tradition links them with Sir Edward Mosley, knight, Attorney General to the Duchy of Lancaster in the early 17th century. This link is confirmed by a deed of 10 October 1655 in which Sir Edward's nephew and heir, Sir Edward Mosley of Rolleston in the county of Staffordshire, baronet, assigned to Gilbert Mosley of Brailsford, gentleman, the remainder of a lease of Bradley Lawnd with its houses, woods, meadows and commons left to him by the Attorney General, subject to the payment to the Receiver of the Duchy of Lancaster of the yearly rent of £4.13.4d. This grant was in consideration of Gilbert's faithful service and other good reasons. Gilbert must have been acting as Sir Edward's agent in some matter but the wording of the consideration hints at some other connection. John Mosley's parentage is not known. Possibly he was a nephew or cousin of Sir Nicholas Mosley, Lord Mayor of London in 1599. Sir Nicholas, a Staffordshire man, who died in 1612 is known to have had two younger brothers, Anthony Mosley of Ancoats and Oswald Mosley of Garret.

Bradley Lawnd, a substantial stretch of grazing land with farm buildings, formerly belonging to the Duchy, lay in Duffield Frith. It must have been a valuable asset to Gilbert Mosley event if his title was disputed by a new purchaser of the freehold in 1670, involving him in a case in Chancery. Gilbert seems to have let this property and continued to farm in Brailsford as a tenant of the Shirley family which he had been since at least 1649. Several bonds amongst his surviving papers and a letter from his son, John, dated 17 September 1671 show him much concerned with undescribed business activities which must have been those of a grazier. John, his younger son known only from this letter, lived in London. After sending his own and his wife's duty to his parents and love to his brother and wife and little one [Jane], he wrote despondently of various bad debts he was trying to collect for his father, and the frustration of his own

purchase of a commission in Customs.

Gilbert Mosley, senior, lost his wife in January 1676. He himself was buried on 8 September 1678 when Jane was nine years old. His son, Gilbert Mosley, junior, succeeded to his father's farm and to judge from his daughter's upbringing to his business as a grazier. He owned some property in Brailsford outright for he sold the blacksmith's shop and croft there in 1672. Jane was carefully educated. A draft letter of 1685 to her uncle still survives asking him to buy for her on her parents' behalf a flowered silk gown, a pink petticoat, a large black hood, a muff, a fan and a gold ring for about £20 because they could buy nothing as modish or as cheap in Derby. A further draft letter acknowledged their receipt and despatched the money. The drafts might be thought an exercise in penmanship but a small enamelled ring set with three tiny diamonds still survives, believed by her descendants to be the ring sent in answer to her letter. A draft bond survives from the same year penned very elaborately in Latin with an English translation and condition. Her recipe book is written in a good clean hand, complete with ornate capital letters, some of which have been used to adorn this edition. She had a firm grasp of the English grammar, and was acquainted with one of the short-hand systems flourishing in the late 17th century. Her erratic spelling means very little because spelling only fossilised with the popularisation of dictionaries in the 18th century. In the early 1690's when she was in her twenties Jane learned to play the violin tolerably well. Her friend, R Barker of Darley, in London on legal business wrote to her on 11 January 1696 regretting that he could not find the 11th edition of Playford's Book on Musique which she had asked him to buy and send her. He could find earlier editions and Purcell's 12th edition, and asked her to let him know quickly which she wanted. Playford's *Brief Introduction to the Skill of Musick for Song and Viol* first appeared in 1658, and Purcell's edition in 1694. Her copy was still in family hands until a couple of years ago. If, as she seems to claim, she wrote the poem about the Spanish lady she must have read and sung a good deal of verse, because it hit popular taste to a nicety. It was current as anonymous verse well into the 18th century, and is even quoted by Georgette Heyer in *The Grand Sophy*.

Jane's standard of living was high. Even if many of her recipes were not for everyday use but rather for entertaining and the more festive occasion they were still verging on the luxurious, with lavish use of wine for cooking, imported oranges, lemons, dried fruits and spices. Some of her medical ingredients were costly. She moved in a circle which understood the importance of pure water, and knew about conduit water, piped water, then found in very few places. She had a recipe for chewett, a term which did not enter the English language until 1688. She owned tiffanies, sarcenets, and silk stockings, fancy points, lace, and other costly items of clothing. Her medical recipes are those of a literate, well-to-do woman of the day, using imported drugs as well as home grown herbs, medical compounds as well as country samples. Sir Edward Terril's salve occurs in other Derbyshire recipe books of the period, and possibly originated in Cheshire where a branch of the Tyrrell or Terril family lived. Dr Willughby's water probably owes its origin to Percival Willughby, 1596-1685. He was a doctor of national standing, a leading obstetrician and writer on obstetrics who practised in London for a time, but spent most of his professional life in Derby. She was not therefore a simple yeoman's daughter. No trace of her family has been found so far amongst dealers in lead, so it is highly probable that her father and grandfather were, like her sons, Gilbert and Roger Soresby, graziers as well as arable farmers.

Jane had more than one admirer. She kept two love letters from William Chatterton, but early in 1697 she married Edward Soresby of Darley. She may have met him through Thomas Mosley, rector of Darley, who died in office in 1685, but more likely she met him through her father's business activities. He was also related to her friend, R Barker. Edward was the third generation of the Darley branch of the Soresby family, which has several branches in the Chesterfield area, including one at Ashover from which the Darley branch possibly sprang. Many men of the Soresby family were active dealers in cattle and lead. Edward was the younger son of Roger Soresby of Toadhole, now Twodales in Darley Dale, born in April 1665. His elder brother died in 1676 and his father in 1693. He was not content to follow his father but set about building up his own estate. In September 1686 he agreed to buy from Katherine Marbury of Darley Hall, widow, for £320 three farms, one of them in Toadhole, the others apparently in the main village. In 1695 he stood surety for John Heydon, his brother-in-law in a bond of £80, securing himself by a further bond of £160 from Heydon to him. It is probable that Heydon could not meet his commitments for at some later date Edward acquired his farm also. To raise £320 even on mortgage and stand surety for so large a sum as £80 Edward himself must have been a grazier. This is borne out by a later survey of his land in Darley which totalled 117 acres, made up of a little more than 9 acres arable and 107 acres of enclosed grazing land.

By 1697 Gilbert Mosley was ready to retire. He had buried his wife Hester on 6 June 1695, and was now anxious to hand his farm and business to Jane and her husband. On 3 February 1697 the arrangements were concluded in three separate deeds. Gilbert gave £200 as Jane's marriage portion. Edward in return settled two farms, four cottages and land in Darley bought from Katherine Marbury as Jane's jointure should she survive him, and after her death in tail male on his sons and their male issue in succession. In return for his keep and £10 yearly Gilbert handed over to Edward the lease of his farm and all his house and farming stock except his wearing apparel and the bed with all its furniture in the parlour. If Gilbert decided to leave the farm he received £10 yearly only. This was secured on a third farm belonging to Edward.

The deed arranging the transfer of the farm listed Gilbert's farming stock which included hay and corn, 4 oxen, 6 cows, a heifer, 6 bullock stirks, 2 heifer stirks, 6 calves, 2 mares, 2 foals, 1 gelt colt, 10 wethers, 21 ewes, 1 ram hog, and 1 swine. This was a large head of livestock to be carrying in the depths of winter in the late 17th century before modern winterfeeding systems were introduced. It points clearly to Gilbert's main interests lying in livestock, and to his business as a grazier.

Jane and Edward must have married very shortly after these settlements. So far as is known Gilbert made his home with them until his death. The parish register is lost for the years between 1695 and 1709, so exact dating is difficult in this period. Gilbert died possibly in 1703 and certainly before 2 March 1704 when his son was cited to exhibit his will. He must have seen all his grandsons: first Gilbert, named for him, who was baptised on 5 January 1698; then Roger, named for Edward's father; then Charles baptised on 23 October 1701. He never saw his grand-daughters: Mary baptised on 25 September 1704 and buried on 9 December next; Jane baptised in 1706; a second Mary baptised on 5 May 1709; and last Frances baptised on 30 January 1712. 1712 was an unhappy year. Sickness hit the family late that autumn. First Jane, Edward's wife, died, aged 43 years. She was buried on 22 October. Then her daughter Jane was buried on 2 November and finally the baby Frances on 6 November.

Edwards was left with three young sons and his eight year old daughter Mary. He did not re-marry. Perhaps his one surviving sister, Frances Heydon, came to help him, or else he managed with servants to run his home and care for his children. This cannot have been easy for a grazier, for business took him away a good deal. All the farmers and other sizeable holders of land in a parish were liable to serve the parish offices of overseer of the poor, churchwarden, and constable, which tied men pretty closely to the parish in the year of office. In Brailsford there was an obligatory rota for office, turns in which could be shifted slightly by arrangement. Gilbert Mosley served his turns as churchwarden and overseer in 1673 and 1675. Edward Soresby served his turns in 1698 and 1699 and again in 1720 and 1722. It was usual for the men liable for office to examine annually the accounts of the officer for the year. Neither Gilbert Mosley concerned himself much with these annual inspection, nor to begin with did Edward Soresby. Before Jane's death he countersigned three sets of accounts. After her death he countersigned one set of accounts in 1714, 1717, 1718, 1719 and 1721, and two sets in 1726 and 1727, almost as if he were making an effort to be more at home and take more part in parish life. From about 1717 he probably received growing help and support from his sons both on the farm and in his business. They must have increasingly shouldered the travelling.

To judge from his first and second wills Edward Soresby was extremely fond of his children and of his one surviving sister, Frances Heydon. Much of his real property was already settled on his eldest son Gilbert under the settlement of 1697, and as eldest son, Gilbert would inherit any other real property not disposed of by will or gift. Edward's first will made in 1721 left the farm bought from John Heydon to his sister Frances for life, then equally between his son Charles and his daughter Mary. To his son Roger he left his little black filly, and 3 outstanding debts. His household goods and furniture were to be divided equally between his children except for 3 gold rings, 2 chests of drawers, a couple of trunks and his wife's clothes which he left to Mary. He left 20s each to his old servants Hannah Peach and Christopher James, and 10s to another servant. The rest of his personal estate he left to Gilbert who was to pay Charles and Mary £125 each.

Mary died in 1722, and in 1729 Edward made another will. Again he left to his very loving sister, Frances, for life the rents of the lands bought from her husband, but this time he divided the reversion between Roger and Charles. He left £150 to Charles in addition to £50 already given to him. His household goods and plate he divided between his three very loving sons, and left all the residue of his estate to Gilbert.

Edward Soresby died in 1732. He was buried on 12 April. His sons, Roger and Gilbert, became the two most respected men in the parish, the only ones to rate the courtesy title Mr before their names in the parish register between 1757 and 1767. Gilbert stayed on in the old farm, and Charles who never married lived with him. Gilbert's account books still survive and show him trading in cattle, mainly locally. He played a great part in parish affairs, not only serving office but regularly countersigning parish accounts. From 1734 to his death in 1755 he missed only the occasional inspection. He married Ann Ford from Ashleyhay and had four children, Edward, who was born in 1742 and died in 1747, Ann born in 1745, Esther born 1747, and Gilbert born in 1750. Jane's recipe book has come down to us through the hand of this last child, and his descendant Frederick Soresby Ogden.

Roger must have set up for himself in his father's lifetime, again almost certainly as a grazier. He took as little part as possible in parish life. Only once did he countersign an important vestry memorandum, and he even arranged to serve his turns as churchwarden and overseer in the same year, 1748. This was a heavy burden and indicates extreme reluctance to be tied too closely to Brailsford for longer than necessary. He must have built up a very thriving business on the fruits of which he and later his son-in-law founded a leading local family. Roger probably married earlier than Gilbert for his first child, Jane, was born in 1736. He had in all five daughters by his wife, Elizabeth

Morley. Only the two eldest lived to be his co-heiresses at his death in 1762. Jane married Edward Chamberlain, a Northamptonshire gentleman, in 1766. Her younger sister Mary, born in 1738, married in 1762 William Cox, aged 20 years. William was the grandson of William Cox who had been tutor to Earl Ferrers' family and lived at Brailsford Parsonage. The tutor's son, a second William, died aged 42 years about 1750 when his son was only 8 years old. Whether William Cox the third was employed by Roger Soresby is not known, but after his marriage to Mary he must have continued Roger's business because he went on to build up a large estate.

Some bitterness seems to have grown up between Jane's grandson, Gilbert Soresby, and William Cox, her grand-daughter's husband. It possibly stems from the difficulties encountered by Gilbert Soresby, senior, and his son in dealing with Edward Soresby's real property. Gilbert, senior, was selling off land in Toadhole as early as 1736. Litigation with Earl Ferrers over the lease of the old Mosley farm in the mid 18th century stretched their resources thinly, but they seem to have managed to buy the farm before 1780 when Gilbert, junior, was owner and occupier of enough land in Brailsford to be rated at £2.15s. in the land tax assessment, a holding of probably about 110 acres. William Cox, described reverently as Mr Cox, was owner-occupier of land assessed at £7.16s.4d, landlord of another parcel assessed at £3.1s.10d., and joint owner of a third parcel assessed at £3.6s. Between them the two owned about a tenth of the parish, bought with the proceeds of the graziers' business set up and continued by Jane Mosley's father and grandfather, and enlarged by her husband,

Edward Soresby. William Cox was apparently conscious of Edward Soresby's contribution to his fortunes, for he named his first child Edward Soresby at his baptism in 1764. William Cox went on to buy the manor of Culland in 1794. Gilbert Soresby found his finances stretched and sold his farm. He remained as a tenant of John Toplis, probably the Wirksworth banker, until as family tradition tells, his landlord sold the farm to William Cox. He refused to be Cox's tenant and moved away. So Jane Mosley's home changed hands again, back into family ownership. The family papers however stayed with Gilbert Soresby, the head of her family, and many still survive in her descendant's hands.

Joan Sinar
Derbyshire County Archivist

The layout of the pages in both the Recipes and Remedies follows the original handwritten manuscript line for line.

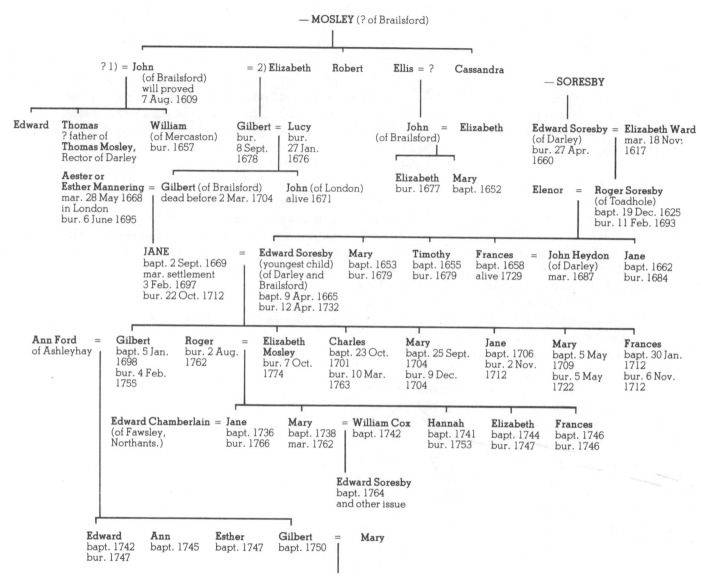

— MOSLEY (? of Brailsford)

? 1) = John (of Brailsford) will proved 7 Aug. 1609   = 2) Elizabeth   Robert   Ellis = ?   Cassandra   — SORESBY

Edward   Thomas ? father of **Thomas Mosley**, Rector of Darley   **William** (of Mercaston) bur. 1657   **Gilbert** bur. 8 Sept. 1678 = **Lucy** bur. 27 Jan. 1676   **John** (of Brailsford) = **Elizabeth**   **Edward Soresby** (of Darley) bur. 27 Apr. 1660 = **Elizabeth Ward** mar. 18 Nov: 1617

Aester or Esther Mannering mar. 28 May 1668 in London bur. 6 June 1695 = **Gilbert** (of Brailsford) dead before 2 Mar. 1704   **John** (of London) alive 1671   **Elizabeth** bur. 1677   **Mary** bapt. 1652   **Elenor** = **Roger Soresby** (of Toadhole) bapt. 19 Dec. 1625 bur. 11 Feb. 1693

JANE bapt. 2 Sept. 1669 mar. settlement 3 Feb. 1697 bur. 22 Oct. 1712 = **Edward Soresby** (youngest child) (of Darley and Brailsford) bapt. 9 Apr. 1665 bur. 12 Apr. 1732   **Mary** bapt. 1653 bur. 1679   **Timothy** bapt. 1655 bur. 1679   **Frances** bapt. 1658 alive 1729 = **John Heydon** (of Darley) mar. 1687   **Jane** bapt. 1662 bur. 1684

Ann Ford of Ashleyhay = **Gilbert** bapt. 5 Jan. 1698 bur. 4 Feb. 1755   **Roger** bur. 2 Aug. 1762 = **Elizabeth Mosley** bur. 7 Oct. 1774   **Charles** bapt. 23 Oct. 1701 bur. 10 Mar. 1763   **Mary** bapt. 25 Sept. 1704 bur. 9 Dec. 1704   **Jane** bapt. 1706 bur. 2 Nov. 1712   **Mary** bapt. 5 May 1709 bur. 5 May 1722   **Frances** bapt. 30 Jan. 1712 bur. 6 Nov. 1712

Edward Chamberlain (of Fawsley, Northants.) = **Jane** bapt. 1736 bur. 1766   **Mary** bapt. 1738 mar. 1762   = **William Cox** bapt. 1742   **Hannah** bapt. 1741 bur. 1753   **Elizabeth** bapt. 1744 bur. 1747   **Frances** bapt. 1746 bur. 1746

Edward Soresby bapt. 1764 and other issue

Edward bapt. 1742 bur. 1747   **Ann** bapt. 1745   **Esther** bapt. 1747   **Gilbert** bapt. 1750 = **Mary**

living descendant, **Frederick Soresby Ogden.**

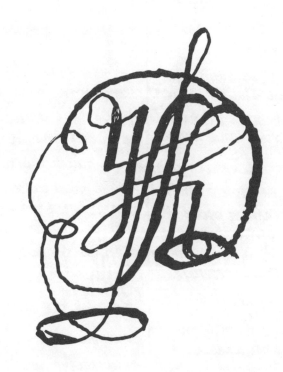

...raisins of the sunne, and put them all in a coffin of fine paste, with a peece of sweet butter, and so bake it: but before you serue it in, cut it up, and wring in the Juyce of an orange and sugar to the meat of stockefish

Boyle watered stockefish, and make it fit to be eaten: when it his cold take the whitest of the fish and mince it small: put in parboyled Currans, raisins of the sunne season it with nutmeg, pepper salt, and a peece of sweet butter bake it but before you serue it in cut, cut it up, and wring in the Juyce of an orange

a Quarter tart of pippins

Quarter them and lay them betweene two sheets of paste: put in apeece of whole sinamon, two or three, bruised cloues, a little sliced, orengado, or onely the yellow outside of the oringe, a bit of sweet butter about the bignesse of an egge

, good store of sugar: sprinkle on a little water then close your tarte, and bake it, Ice it before it goe to the board, serue it hot this tart you may make of any puff, or short paste that will not hold the raysing if you bake in any of these kindes of paste, then you must first boyle your pippens in claret wine and sugar, or else your apples will be hard wen your crust will be burnt and dryed away besides, the wine giueth them a pleasant colour, and a good taste allso though you boyle your pippens tender, take heed you breake not the quarters, but bake them whole

Gooseberry tart

Pick the stalkes of your gooseberries and the pips int the tops put them i good paste, with a little greene ginge sliced in slices: cast on good store of sugar and rose water, and so close them

To roast a neates tongue on the french fashion

Chop sweet hearbes fine, with a Peece of raw apple, season it with pepper, Ginger and the yolke of a new Laid egge chopt small to mingle among it. Then stuffe it well with that farcing and so roast it. The sawce for it is verjuyce butter, and the juyce of a lemmon and a little nutmegge. Let the tongue lye in the sawce when it goeth to the table. Garnish your dish as you thinke fittest or as you are furnisht.

A way to boyle Chickens or pigeons with gooseberryes or grapes

Boyle them with mutton broth and white wine, a peece of whole mace. Put into the bellies of them sweet hearbs. When they be tender thicken it with a peece of manchet and two hard egge yolkes strained with some of the same broth. Then put some of the same broth into a boyldmeat dish

1

with veriuyce, butter, and sugar, and so boyle your grapes or gooseberries in the dish close covered, till they be tender, and poure it on the breast of your dish.

To boyle a Chine of mutton or veale in sharpe broth on the french fashion

Cover your meate with faire water and a little white wine, a peece of whole mace, a nutmeg quartered, a handfull of hearbs cleane pickt, and bruised with the backe of a ladle, young lettice spinage, parsley, tops of young time. When all is boyled well together, thicken it with a crust of manchet, and the yolke of a hard egge, steeped in some of the same broth, and draw it through a strainer, and thicken your broth with it. Season it with a little veriuyce and pepper.

To boyle larkes or sparrowes

Trusse them fit to boyle and put them into a pipkin, with a ladlefull of mutton broth, a peece of whole mace, a quarter of a nutmegge, a fagot of sweet hearbes, and a little young parsley picket cleane and short: put your parsley loos into you broth: season it with veriuyce, pepper and sugar. Thicken it with the yolkes of two new laid egges hard and a peece of manchet, strained with some of the same broth, till they be tender. Garnish your dish as you will.

Baked Meates

A made dish of coney livers

Parboyle three or foure of them, and then chop them fine with sweet hearbes, the yolkes of two hard egs, season it with sinamon, ginger and nutmeg and pepper: put in a few parboyld currans and a little melted butter, and so make it up into little pastyes, frye them in a frying pan.

Shave on sugar, and serve them to the bord.

A made dish of a sweet bread

Boyle, or roast your sweet bread, and put into it a few parboyld currans, a minst date, the yolkes of two new laid egges, a peece of manchet grated fine, season it with a little pepper, salt, nutmeg and sugar, wring in the juyce of an oarnge or lemmon, and put it betweene two sheets of puf paste, or any other good paste and eyther bake it, or fry it, whether you please.

A made dish of sheepes tongues

Boyle them tender, and slice them in thin slices: then season them with sinamon, ginger, and a little pepper and put them into a coffin of fine paste, with sweet butter, and a few sweet hearbes chopt fine: bake them in an oventhen take a little nutmeg, vinegar, butter, sugar, the yolke of a new layd egge, one spoonful of sacke, and the juyce of a lemmon: boyle all these together on a chafing dish of coales and put it into your pye: shog it well together and serve it to the table.

A Florentine of a cony, the wing of a Capon, or the kidny of veale

Mince any of these with sweet hearbes, parboyled currans, a date or two minst small, a peece of a preserved orange or lemmon, minst as small as your date. Season it with ginger, sinamon, nutmeg and sugar: then take the yolkes of two new laid egges, a spoonefull of sweet creame, a peece of short cake grated and marrow cut in short peces. Bake this in a dish betweene two leaves of puf paste. Put a little rose water to it before you close your paste. When it is baked shave on sugar.

A frydayes pye without either flesh or fish

Wash greene beets cleane, picke out the middle string, and chop them small with two or three well relisht ripe apples. Season it with pepper, salt and ginger: then take a good handfull of raisins of the sunne, and put them all in a coffin of fine paste, with a peece of sweet butter, and so bake it: but before you serve it in, cut it up, and wring in the Juyce of an orange and sugar.

A Chewet of stockfish

Boyle watered stockefish, and make it fit to be eaten: when it his cold take the whitest of the fish and mince it small: put in parboyled Currans, raisins of the sunne. Season it with nutmeg, pepper, salt and a peece of sweet butter. Bake it but before you serve it in, cut it up, and wring in the Juyce of an orange.

A Quarter tart of pippins

Quarter them and lay them between two sheets of paste: put in a peece of whole sinamon, two or three, bruised cloves, a little sliced, orengado, or onely the yellow outside of the oarnge, a bit of sweet butter about the bignesse of an egge,

good store of sugar: Sprinkle on a little rose water then close your tarte, and bake it. Ice it before it goe to the boord, serve it hot. This tart you may make of any puf paste or short paste that will not hold the raysing. If you bake in any of these kindes of pastes, then you must first boyle your pippens in claret wine and sugar, or else your apples will be hard wen your crust will be burnt, and dryed away besides, the wine giveth them a pleasant colour, and a good taste allso. Though you boyle your pippens tender, take heed you breake not the quarters, but bake them whole.

A Gooseberry tart

Pick the stalkes of your gooseberries and the pips in the tops. Put them in goode paste, with a little greene ginger sliced in slices: cast on good store of sugar and rose water, and so close them.

A Cherry pye

Bruise a pound of Cherries, and stamp them, and boyle the sirrup with sugar. Then take the stones out of two pound: bake them in a set coffin. Ice them, and serve them hot in to the boord.

To make an oyster pye

Save the liquor of your largest oysters, season them with pepper and ginger, and put tem into a coffin: put in a minst onyon, a few corrans, and a good peece of butter, then poure in your sirrup and close it. When it is bakt, cut up the pye, and put in a spoonfull of winegar and melted butter: Shake it well together and set it againe into the oven a little while: then take it out and serve it in.

To bake neates tongue to be eaten hot

Boyle it tender, and pill off the skin, take the flesh out at the butt end. Mince it small with oxe suet and marrow and season it with pepper, salt, nutmegge, parboild currans, and a minced date cut in peeces. Take the yolkes of two new laid eggs and a spoonefull of sweet creame, worke all together with a silver spoone in dish, with a little powder of a dryed orange pill: sprinkle a little veriuyce over it, and cast on some sugar. Then thrust it in againe as hard as you can cram it. Bake it on a dish in the oven: baste it with sweet butter that it may not bake dry on the outside. When it is to be eaten sawce it with vinegar and butter, nutmeg, sugar and the juyce of an orange.

To make an umble pye, or for want of umbles to doe it with a lams head and purttenance

Boyle your meat reasonable tender, take the flesh from the bone, and mince it small with beefe suet and marrow with the liver, lights and heart, a few sweet hearbes and currans. Season it with pepper, salt and nut nutmeg: bake it in a coffin raised like an umble pye, and it will eate so like unto umbles, as that you shall hardly by taste discern it from right umbles.

To bake a Calve's Chalderon

Parboyle it, and coole it and pick out the kernels, and cut it in small peeces: then season it with pepper, salt and nutmeg: put in a few sweet hearbs chopt, a peece of sweet buttr, sprinckle it with veriuyce and so close it. When you serve it in, put to it a little of a Cawdle, made with nutmeg, vinegar, butter, sugar and the yolkes of two new laid egs, a spoone full of sacke and the Juyce of an orange.

To bake Eeles

Cut your Eeles about the length of your finger: season them with pepper, salt, and ginger, and so put them into a Coffin, with a good peece of sweet butter. Put into your pye great raisins of the sun, and an onyon minst small, and so close it and bake it.

To bake Chickens with Grapes

Trusse and scald your Chickens, season them well with pepper, salt and nutmeg: and put them into your pye with a good peece of butter; bake it and cut it up, and put upon the breast of your chickens, grapes, boild in verjuyce, butter, nutmeg and sugar, with the Juyce of an orange.

To make a pippin pye

Take their waight in sugar, and sticke a whole clove in every peece of them, and put in peeces of whole sinamon, then put in all your sugar with a slice or two of whole ginger: sprinkle rose water on them before you close your pye: bake them and serve them in.

To bake a Swan

Scald it, and take out the bones: then parboyle it and season it well with pepper, salt and ginger. Then lard it, and put it in a deepe coffin of rye paste, with store of butter. Let it soake well. When you take it out of the oven put in more butter moulten at the vent-hole.

To bake a turkey or a Capon

Bone the turkey but not the capon. Parboyle them, and sticke cloves in their breats: lard them and season them well with pepper and salt, and put them in a deepe coffin with the breast downeward, and store of butter: and when it is bakt, poure in more butter: and when it is cold, stop the vent-hole with more butter.

To bake a wild goose, or mallard

Parboyle them, and breake the brest bone of a large gooce or take it qite out, and all the other bones also but not out of a mallard. Season them and lard them, and put them into a deepe coffins, with store of butter: when you draw them out of the oven, put in more butter and set it into the oven againe to soake: when it is cold stop the hole with butter.

To bake a Curlew or hearneshaw

Trus them and parboyle them, but upon one side season them with pepper, salt and ginger: put them in deepe coffins with store of butter and let the heads hang out for a show.

To bake woodcockes, or blackbrds

Trusse, parboyle, and season them with pepper and salt: your woodcocke may be larded: doe as in other.

To bake Larkes or sparrowes

Serve them as before was shewed in the woodcockes and blacke-birds.

To make panc(a)kes so crispe that you may set them upright

Make a dozen or a score of them in a little frying pan, no bigger than a sawcer, and then boyle them in lard, and they will looke as yellow as gold, beside the taste will be very good.

A sallet of rose buds and clove gilly floweres

Picke rose buds, and put them into a earthen pipkin, with white wine vinegar and sugar: so may you use cowslips, violets, or rose-mary flowers.

To keepe greene cucumbers all the yeare

Cut the cucumbears in peeces, boyle them in spring-water, sugar, and dill, a walnut or two: take them up and let your pickle stand untill it be cold.

To keepe broome capers

Boyle the greatest and hardest buds of the broome in wine vinegar and bay salt, scum it cleane: when it is cold you may put in raw ones also, each by themselves: put in a peele of lead* on the raw ones, for all that swim will be black and the other that are pressed downe, as greene as any leeke. The boyld ones will change colour.

Purslaine stalkes

Gather them at the full growth, but not too old: parboyle them, and keep them in white wine vinegar and sugar.

To make caper rowlers of radish cods

Take them when they be hard, and not overmuch open: boyle them tender in faire water, boyle white wine vinegar and bay salt together, and keep them in it.

The lead referred to is a toxic substance and should not be used

8

Divers sallets boyled

Parboyle spinage, and chop it fine, with the edges of two hard trenchers upon a bord, or the backes of two choppin knives: then set them on a chafin dish of coales with butter and vinegar. Season it with sinamon, ginger, sugar and a few parboyled currans. Then cut hard egges into quarters to garnish it withall, and serve it upon sippets. So may you serve burrage, buglosse, endiffe, suckery, coleflowers, sorrel, marygold leaves, water cresses, leekes, boyled onions, sporragus, rocket, alexanders. Parboyl them and season them all alike: whether it be with oyle and vinegar, or butter and vinegar, sinamon, ginger, sugar and butter: egges are necessary, or at least very good for all boyld sallets.

Buds of hoppes

Seethe them with a little of the tender stalkes in faire water, and put them in a dish over coakes, with butter, and so serve them to the table.

A sallet of mallowes

Strip of the leaves from the tender stalkes saving the tops: let them lye in water, and seete them tender, and put them in a dish over coles, with butter and vinegar: let them stand a while: then put in grated bread and sugar betweene every layr.

A sallet of burdocke rootes

Cut of the outward rinde and lay them in water a good houre at the least: when you have done seeth them untill they be tender: then set them on coales with butter and vinegar, and so let them stand a pretty while, then put in grated bread and sugar, betwixt every layr, and serve them in.

To make blancht manchet in a frying pan

Take halfe a dosen egges, halfe a pinte of sweet creame, a penny manchet grated, a nutmegge grated, two spoonefuls of rose water, two ounces of sugar, worke all stiffe like a pudding. Then frye it like tansey in a very little frying pan that it may be thicke: frye it browne and turne it out upon a plate. Cut it in quarters and serve it like a pudding. Scrape on sugar.

Puddings

A swan or goose pudding

Stirre the blood of a swan, or gooce. Steepe fine oatmeale in milke, nutmeg, pepper, sweet hearbs, minst suet. Mingle all together with rose water, lemmon pill minst fine, coriander seeds, a little quantity thereof. And this is a rule both for grated bread pudding or any other pudding that is made in a swanne or gooce necke.

A rice pudding

Steepe it in faire water all night. Then boyle it in new milke, and draine out the milke through a culliender: mince beefe suet handsomely, but not too small, and put it in the rice, and par boild currans, yolkes of new layd egges, nutmeg, sinamon, sugar and barberies: mingle all together: wash your scoured guts, and stuffe them with the aforesaid pulp: parboyle them, and let them coole.

To make some Kick shawes in paste to fry or bake in what forme you please

Make some sort puff past, rowle it thinn, if you have any moulds you may worke it upon your moulds, with the pulp of pippens, seasoned with sinamon, ginger, sugar and rose water, close them up and bake them or fry them or you may fill them with gooseberries seasoned with sugar, sinamon, ginger and nutmeg. Rowle them up in yolks of egges, and it will keepe your marrow, being boyld, from melteing away, or you may fill them with curds boyled up with whites of egges and creame,

and it will have a tender curde but you
must season the curde with parboyld currans,
three or foure sliced dates put into it, or sixe
bits of marrow as bigge as half a walnut:
put in some small peeces of almond paste,
sugar, rose water and nutmeg and this
will serve for any of these Kickshawes
eyther to bake, or for a florentine
in puft paste: any of these you may fry
or bake, for dinner or supper.

To make an Italian pudding
Take a pinny white Lofe, pare of the crust,
and cut it in square peeces like unto
great dyce, mince a pound of beefe
suet small: take halfe a pound of raisins
of the sunne, stone them and mingle
them together and season with sugar,
rose water and nutmeg, wet these
things in foure egs and stir them
very tenderly for breaking the bread:
then put it in a dish and pricke in three
or foure peeces of marrow, and
some sliced dates: put it into an oven
hot enough for a chewet: if your
oven be too hot, it will burne, if too
cold it will bee heavy. When it is baked

scrape on sugar and serve it hot at
dinner, but not at supper.

To boyle chickens in white broth
Trusse and parboyle them very white.
Then put them with sweet hearbs in
to a pipkin with mace, peeces of sinamon.
Chop a little parsley but cours, and
straine the yolkes of foure or five egges with
a little veriuice, which must be put in when
they are ready to be taken from the fire.
Garnish your dish.

To boyle a rabbet
Parboyle your rabbet well, and cut it in peeces:
then take strong broth, and a fagot of hearbs,
a little parsley, sweet marjoram, three or
foure yolkes of egs strained with a little
white bread, and put all in a pipkin with
mace, cloves and a little veriuyce to make
them have a taste.

To boyle a rabbet with grapes or gooseberries
Trusse your rabbet whole, and boyle it with
strong broth, untill it be ready. Then take
a pinte of white wine, a good handfull
of spinnage chopt in peeces, the yolkes
of egges cut in quarters and a little

large mace: let all boyle together with a fagot of sweet hearbs, and a good peece of butter.

To boyle sawceges

Put them into a quarte of claret wine, large mace, baberries, sinamon, a handfull of sweete hearbes. Garnish this dish with sinamon, ginger, and fine sugar.

To boyle Goose giblets or swannes giblets

Picke and parboyle them cleane and put to them some strong broth with onyons, currans, and parsley and let all boyle together with large mace and pepper: boyle them well with a fagot of sweet hearbes, and then put in verjuyces and butter.

To make pufpaste

Take a quart of floure, a pound and a halfe of sweet butter, worke half a pound of the butter into the floure drie, betwixt your hands, then breake into the floure foure egges, and as much faire water as will wet it, to make it reasonable like paste, then worke it into a peece of a foot long, strew a little floure on the table that it hang not to, then take it by the end, and beat it well about the board untill it stretch long, and then double it, and taking both ends in your hand beate it againe, and do so five or sixe times, then take the other pound of butter, and cut it in thin slices, and spred it all over the one halfe of your paste, with youre thumbe. Then turne the other halfe over your buttered side and turne in the sides round about underneath, then crush it downe with a roling pin and so worke it five or sixe times with your butter, then you may rowle it broad and cut it in foure quarters, and if it be not thin enough rowle it thinner in round peeces, about the thickness of your little finger: then take a dish as broad as your peece of paste, and strow on a little floure on the dish, then lay on one peece of paste, and you may put into it peeces of marrow and hartichoake bottomes, or potato, or eringus rootes: but you must rowle your lumpes of marrow in the yolkes of raw egs, and season them with sinamon, sugar, ginger and a very little salt: lay this upon your paste then lay your other sheete upon that dish, and close it round about the brim of your dish, with your thumbe: then cut off your round with a knife close by the brim of the dish. Then you may cut it crosse the brim of the dish like virginall keyes, and turne them crosse over one another: then bake them in an oven as hot as for small pyes. In this maner you may make florentines of rice, with yolkes of egges boyled with creame: then you may season it with sugar, sinamon and a little nutmeg, three or fore sliced dates, put into it three or foure peeces of almond paste, five or sixe lumps of marrow, stirre them up together, and put them into the florentine, then bake it in an oven, as hot as for pies. If you have rice, boile it tender in milke, and a bleade or two of mace, boyle it untill the milke be byled away. Then season it with a little nutmeg, sinamon, and sugar, two or three raw egges, a little salt, a little rosewater, a handfull of Currans, three or foure sliced dates: you may put this in your dish, betwixt two sheets of puft past and bake it as before. If you have none of these, then you may take quarters of pippins, or pears, the coares taken out, and byled tender in Claret wine, then put them into the paste, or for want of these, you may take Gooseberries, Cherries, or damsons, or apricockes without the stones, or prunes: when you see your paste rise up white in the oven and begin to turne yellow, then take it forth and wash it with rose-water and butter, (s)crape on fine sugar, and set it into the oven againe, about a quarter of an houre, then draw it forth, and serve it in.

To make a Liverie pudding

Boyle a hagges liver very drie, when it is cold grate it, and take as much grated manchet as Liver, sift them thorow a course sive or collender, and season it with cloaves, mace, sinamon and as much nutmeg as of all the other, halfe a pound of sugar, a pound and a halfe of currans, halfe a pinte of rose water, two pound of beefe suet minst small, eight egges, put away the whites of foure: temper your bread and liver with these egges, and rose water, and as much sweet cream as will make it some-thing stiffe: then cut the small guts of a hogge, aboute a foot long, fill them about three quarters full of the aforesaid stuffe. Tie both ends together and boyle them in a kettle of faire water, with a pewter dish under them, with the bottome upward, and it will keepe youre puddings from breaking: when the water seetheth put in your puddings, let them boyle softly a quarter of an houre, and take them up: and so you may keep them in a drie trug a weeke or more: when you spend them you must broyle them.

To make rice puddings

Boyle halfe a pound of rice with three pintes of milke, a little beaten mace, boyle it untill your rice be drie but never stirre it, but if you chaunce to stirr it then you must stirre it continually or else it will burne: poure youre rice into a collinder or else into a strainer that the moisture may runne cleane from it. Then put to it six egges and put away the whites of three, halfe a pound of sugar, a quarter of a pinte of rose-water, a pound of currans, a pound of beefe suet shred small. Season it with nutmeg, sinamon and a little salt. Stirre all this together with a spoone thinne, drie the smallest guts of a hog in a faire cloth being watered and scoured fit for the puddings, and fill them three quarters full, and tie both ends together, let them boyle softly a quarter of an houre or sca[r]ce so much, and let the water boyle before you put them in, and doe as in the other pudding last spoken of.

Christall Gellie

Take a knuckle of veale and a paire or two of Calves feete. Take out the fat beteene the clease, wash them in two or three warme waters and let them be all night in an earthen pot or panne, in faire water. Then next day boyle them very tender in faire spring water, from a gallon to three pintes: then let the liquor stand untill it be cold in an earthen bason, pare away the top

and bottome, and put to it a little rose
waa, season it with double refined
sugar, then put to it halfe dozen
spoonfulls of oyle of sinamon, and
as many of oyle of ginger, and
halfe so much oyle of nutmeg, a
graine of muske tyed in a little
lawne: when all this is boyled
together, put it into a silver or earthen
dish and so let it stand untill
it be thoroughly cold, and then
ether serve it in slices or otherwise,
as you please.

To make gellie of pippins of the clour of amber

Take eight faire pippens, take out
the coares, boyle them in a quart
of spring water, from a quart
unto a pinte. Put in a quarter of
a pinte of rose water, a pound of
fine sugar, and boylee it uncovered
untill it com to the
colour of amber. You may know
when it is enough, by letting a drop
fall on a peece of glasse, and if
it stand it is enough: then let

it rune into an earthen or silver
bason upon a chafin dish of coales
and while it is warme, fill
your boxes or printing moulds with
a spoone and let it stand, and when
it is cold you may turne it out of your
mould, and it will be printed on the
upper side.

To make Gellie of pippens as orient red as a rubie

Take eight faire pippens, take out
the coares, boyle them in a quart of
spring water, and a pound of fine
sugar, boyle it still covered close
untill it be red, and in all the other
operations you must doe as in the
amber coloured gellies, remembring
alwaies that your boxe or mouldes
bee laid in water before you use
them three or foure hours, and the
gellie will not cleave unto them.

To make white Leach of Almonds

Take halfe a pound of Jordan almonds,
lay them in cold water, the next
day blanch them, and beate them
in a stone morter, put in som damaske
rose-water in to the beating
of them: and when they be beaten
very fine, draw them trough

a strainer, with a quart of sweet milke, from the Cow: set it upon a Chafing dish of Coales, with a peece of Isinglas, a peece of whole mace, one nutmeg quartered, a graine of muske of tyed in a faire clout and hung upon a thread in it: and when you see grow (recipe unfinished)

To stew beef

Take a good rump of beef, cut from the bones, shred turnips and Carrots, small, and spinage, and Lettce, put all in a pan, and let it stew 4 hours with so much water, and a quart of white wine as will cover it, when it is stewed enough then put in a glassfull of elder vinegar, and serve it in with sippets.

How to stew steaks between two dishes

You must put parsly, Currans, butter, verjuice, and 2 or 3 yolks of egges, pepper, cloves and mace, and so let them boil together, and serve them upon sops. Likewise you may do steaks of mutton or beef.

How to stew calves feet

Boil them, and blanch them, cut them in two, and put them into a pipkin with strong broth, then put in a little powder of seffron, and sweet butter, pepper, sugar, and some sweet herbs finely minced. Let them stew an hour, put in salt and save them.

To preserve oranges

Take a pound of oranges, and a pound of sugar, pill the outward rind, and inward white skin off, take juice of oranges, put them into the juice, boil them half an hour, and take them off.

To make Cimbals

Take fine flower dried, and as much Sugar as flower, then take as much whites of egges as will make it paste, and put in a little rose-water, then put in a quantity of coriander seed, and annise seeds, then mold it up in that fashion you will bake it in.

To make sugar Cakes

Take one pound of fine flower, 1 pound of sugar finely beaten, and mingle them well together. Then take 7 or 8 yolks of eggs, and if your flower be good take a white or two as you shall think good, take 2 cloves and a pretty piece of cinamon, and lay it in a spoonful of rose-water all night, and heat it almost blood warm. Temper it with the rest of the stuff, when the paste is made up. Make it up with as much haste as you can, bake them in a soft oven.

To make cakes of lemons or violets

Take of the finest double refined sugar, beaten very fine, and searced through a fine tiffany, and to half a silver porringer of sugar, put to it two spoonfuls of water, and boil it till it be almost sugar again, then grate of the hardest rinded lemon, then stir it into your sugar, put it into your coffins or paper, and when they be cold, take them off.

To candy all kind of fruitages, as oranges Lemons, citrons, Lettice stocks, sugar candys, such as the comfit-makers do candy the fruits with

Take 1 pound of refined sugar and put it into a posnet with as much water as will wet it, and so boil it till it come to a candy cight [state?], then take all your fruit-being preserved and dried, then draw them through your hot sugar, and then lay them on your hurdle, and in one quarter of one hour they will be finely candied.

To do clove Gilliflowers up for salleting all the year

Take as many clove-gilliflowers as you please, slip off the leaves. Then strow some sugar in the bottom of the gally pot that you do them in, and then a lane [layer] of gilliflowers, and then a lane of sugar, and so do until all the gilliflowers be done, then pour some claret wine into them, as much as will cover them, then cut a peece of a thin board, and lay it on them to keep them dowen, then tye them close and set them in the sun, and let them stand a month, or thereabouts, but keep them from any rain or wet.

To stew sausages

Boil them in fair water and salt a little,
for sauce boil some currans alone,
when they be almost tender, then pour out
the water and put in a little whit wine,
butter and sugar.

To make curd cakes

Take a pint of curd, four eggs, take out
2 of the whites, put in some sugar, a
little nutmeg, and a little flower,
stir them well together, and drop
them in, and fry them with a little
butter.

How to candy pears, plumbs, or apricocks, that they shall look as clear as any

Take your apricocks or plumbs and give every
one a cut to the stone in the notch, and then
cast sugar on them, and bake them in an
oven as hot as for manchet close stopped, bake
them in an earthen platter, let them stand
half an hour, then take them out of the
dish, and lay them one by one upon glass
plates, and so dry them: if you can get
glasses made like marmalet boxes to lay
over them, they will be the sooner candied:
this is the manner to cady any such fruit.

To make ponado

The quantity you will make set on in a
posnet of faire water, when it boils,
put a mace in, and a little piece
of Cinnamon, and so much bread as
you think meet, so boil it, and season
it with salt, sugar, and rose water,
and so serve it.

To Make a Caudle

Take ale the quantity that you mean to
make, and set it on the fire, and when
it is ready to boil, scum it very
well, then cast in a large mace, and
take the yolks of 2 eggs for 1 mess or
one drought and beat them well, and
take away the skin of the yolks, and
then put them into the ale, when
it seetheth. Be sure to stir them well
till it seeth again for a youngling,
then let it boil a while and put in
your sugar, and if it be to eat cut
three or four toasts of bread
thin, and toast them dry but not
brown, and put them to the Caudle,
if to drink put none.

[To prevent constipation]
(unlabelled recipe)
Take half an ounce of good
Rubarb and 1 ounce of turmricke
and 4 peniworth of
Jollap and pound them all
into a fine powder so fine
as to go thorrow a hare
or a lawn fines(t) and tak
1 ounce of anni seeds: and
1 peniworth of senee. Dri
them and pound them
into as fine a powder as the
other and then take 1 ounce
of the Creame of tartar and
then tak 1 pound of good
Currans and wash them and
dry them with a linen Cloth
and then pound them: and then
pound all the pouders with
them and when they are all
well mixed put it into a poot
and then put thes syrups into
it thus
syrup of suttory with ruborb
1 ounce syrup of roses solutire
[?solution] 1 ounce

syrup of buckethorne 1 ounce
Mix the syrups together and
mix the syrups weell with the
rest of the things and
take every night as much
of it as 5 or 6 or 7 [?pennyweights]
and take as much every morning
and drink a drought
of warm ale after it every
night and morning: and a
drought of ale or poset drink
after every stool: and eate
your diner: you ma[y] take more
or les of it as you see it
worketh with you.

How to make the pectorall infusion

Tak one pinte and a halfe
of white wine and put 1 quarte
of spring water to it
and put them both into an Earthen
Jugg and then put these
things into them thus: salt of
tartar half an ounce, Cream

of tartar in powder halfe an
ounce, Spanish Juice of
Liquorise 3 ounce, golden maden
hare 2 peniworth, seall
2 peniworth, anniseeds 1
ounce. Pound the seeds and
take 2 ounces of Liquoricies
Scrap it and slice it and put
all into the Jugg and stop it
close up and keep it hot by
the fire 24 or 26 and keep
the Cleare liquor in bottels
and take of it Every night 6 or 7
spoonefulls wormed [warmed], and
so much in a morning, and so
much at 4 in the afternoon.
You should put into it 1 pound
of rasins o the son at the
first but you must take all
the stones out of them before
but this in summer the will
caues it to sower but if you
mak it with raisins you need
not put in the Liqoriaes scraped
nor but 2 ounces of the spanish
Juyce: and when you have

strained out the firest lickor put 3 pints of spring water to the ingrediens agane into the Jugg and keep it hot by the fiere 24 or 26 houres and then sraine it hard out and keep it by itselfe. It will be good to drink a good drought of it night and morning warmed but not so good as the firest.

To Make Goosbery [wine]

Take your wine gooseberys very ripe and picke them Cleane. Then bruise them in a marble morter or in a wooden basin with a wooden pestle. To every gallon of fruite tak a gallon of Spring water well boyled and skumed. Then put the fruite and water into an earthen pot. So let them stand Close Covered

fore hours to infuse. Then let them draine through a haire sive and to the Cleare liquer put for each gallon of fruit two pounds of good lumpe sugar. Soo put the liquer and sugar into an earthen pot Close Covered and set it in a seller for a moneth. Then open it and take of the skume and bottle soe much of it as is Cleare and to every quarte bottle put two ounces of sugar. Corke them and tye them close up and set them into a Cool seller. This wine will be good and briske at 2 moneths ould: so well for a yeare. This receat will serve as well for Corans, resbereys or Strawberryes and with many other fruits onely Cherries.

To make raison wine

Take 6 pound of raisons, 2
quarts of water well boyled
as long as any skum is to be
taken of as it riseth. Your
raisens must be well washed
and stoned and put
into a pot that hath a
Spigot and forset and
two lemons and one
pound of lompe sugar.
Take one rine of[f] and put
them both in the pot thin
sliced and put the water
boyling hot upon these before
named and let it stand
4 or 5 dayes. Then draine
it thoroug a haire sive and
when it is cleare bottle
it up with a pound of lump
sugar, into every bottle
2 or 3 lumps.
This is the
true way to mak Couslip
wine allsoe. You may set
your bottles when filed

two or 3 days in the sun.
This I have seen Mrs
Powell doe. You may try
som soe and put them
in a sellar after with the rest.

To make Cherry wine

Take 5 pounds of sugar, one quart of
water. Boyle it a little. Skum it cleane.
Then put in 14 pounds of Cherrys stoned
besides the iuyce that comes from them.
Boyle them for three quarters of an
houre: skum them often and cover them
as the boyle with a long sheet of white
paper that the sugar may boyle all
over them. Then power them into
earthen pans, and let them stand
24 hours. After take out the cherrys
and put them upon sives to draine
for 6 hours: then strow loafe sugar
fine beaten on the toppes of the
sives you dry them upon and lay the
Cherryes on. Then strew sugar upon
the cherries. Dry them in the son
and turn them som times: the
Juyce from which you take your
Cherrys that is to make your wine.
It must stand in the pans for 8 or 10 dayes.
Then strain it through an hipachrist bagg into a small
runlett or bottles every night and
morning till the wine hath done
working and be very cleare on the top.
Then stop it up close and keep it in a
cool sellar. It will be ready to drink in September
but you may keep it all winter.

To make raison wine
take 6 pound of raisones 20
quarts of water well boyled
as long as any skum is to be
taken of as itt riseth your
raisens must be well was
hed and stoned and put
into a pot that hath a
spigott and forsett and
two lemons and put one
pound of lompe sugar
take one rine of and put
them both in the pot thin
sliced and put the water
boyling hot upon these be
named and let it stand
4 or 5 dayes then draine
it throrow a haire sive and
when it is cleare bottle
it up with a pound of lump
sugar into every bottle
2 or 3 lumps

This is the
true way to make Cousin
wine allsoe you may set
your bottles when filled

two or 3 dayes in the sun
this Cleare then in
pane See you may try
som soe and put them
in a Glass as after with
ye rest

To make Cherry wine

take 5 pounds of sugar one quart of
water boyle it a litle skum it Cleare
then put in 14 pounds of Cherrys stoned
besides the juyce that comes from them
boyle them for three quarters of an
houre: skum them often and Couer them
as the boyle with a long sheet of white
paper that the sugar may boyle all
ouer them then power them into
earthen pans and let them stand
24 hours after take out the Cherrys
and put them upon siues to draine
for 6 hours: then strow lowe sugar
fine beaten on the toppes of their
siues you dry them upon and lay the
cherrys on then strew sugar upon
the Cherries and them in the sonn
and turn them som times: the
Juyce from which you take your
Cherrys that is to make your wine
it must stand in the pans for 8 or 10
dayes then strain it through an
hipacrist bagg into a small
runnlet or bottles every night and
morning till the wine hath done
wyrking and be very cleare on the top
then stop it up close and keep it in a
Cellar it will be ready to drink in septem
but you may keep it all winter

Recipes

mi · love unto mi · ffrend

Remedies

This ring is round and hath no ...

to get the ~~spots~~ steins of ~~fruit~~
fruits out of any linen coth

take them be4 the are washed :-
with a ~~~~ bitter rub every spot
well: then let / cloth lie • scald
hot ~~water~~ milk a while — when it
is a ~~~~ cool: rub / spott, paces • /
milk till you see / are quite out!
— then wash it • water — soap

    to take out any greasie spots
out of silk stuff or cloth
take a linen ~~~~ Ray — wet it wery well
• fare water: then with a pare of tongs
put a ~~~~ liue sea cole or wood coal upon
/ rag :— hastily close / rest of / rag
about / cole :— presently lay it upon
/ greasie spot whilst it is smak ~~~~
:— when you perceive it to cool do s
again :— so do till you find / spots are
quite taken out : How to make Clean pa,
wash your plate first • soap suds dry
it: then if there be any spots sub them
out with salt — Vinegar. then anint
your plat all over with ~~~~ ar —
Chalk: then lay it • / ~~~~ or be4 / fire
to dry: then rub it of with warm
linen Cloths: very well — it will
look like ~~~~ new

1. ⁿ⁄₇ / ℄

there is no best thing to wash / ℄ with
: to keep it smoot — 1. scower it clean
.. than to wash it every —4 with bran
dy: wherein you haue steeped a ~~~~ flow
er of brimstone :— / next day wib it
only with a Cloth

    1. mak a salue for / lips

take two ounces of whit bees wax :—
slice it thin: then melt it ouer / sire
with two ounces of salet oyl :— a ~~~~ whit
sugar Candi :— when you see it well in
corporat, take it of / fire — let it stand
till it is coed: then set / skillet on / fire
aggne: till / bottom is warm — so turn it
out: anoint your lips or ~~son~~ sore nose:
or sore nipples with this :— it will heal
them

    to keep / teeth Clean — sound

take Common white salt one ounce: as
much Curtle bone: beat them together —
rub your teeth with them eucry morn
— then wash them with fair water

    1. ~~~~ / hp ⁷⁄ — ¹⁄

take daffadil • clean water till it
grow ~~~~ then put thereto powder of
Cantariun — stir them together: put
thereto two eggs — stir them well
together :— with this ointment anint your
hands :— within 3 or 4 days yse thereof
will be whit, / clear — soft

one nutmeg and a littel salt.
Worke it very well, and let it
stand half an our by the fire,
and then woork it againe,
and then make it up and
let it stand an our and
halfe in the oven; let
not the oven be too hot.

Y

12   It cuereth biles, blanes, botches, impostomes, swelings and tumours in any part of the body.

13   It helpeth all aches and paines of the genitours in man or woman.

14   It cureth scabs, itch, and wrenches, sprains, strains, gouts, palsies, dropsies and waters betwen the flesh and skin.

15   It healeth the hemorrhoides or piles in man or woman.

16   It cureth the bloody flux if the belly be anointed there with.

17   Make a sear cloth thereof to heal all the above said maladies with very many other, which for brevety sake are omited.

Ar kings way to make mead

Take five quarts and a pint of water and warm it, then put one quart of honey to every gallon of liquor, one lemmon, and a quarter of an ounce of motmegs [nutmegs]; it must boyel till the scuem rise black, that you will have it quickly ready to drink, squeeze into it limon when you ton it. It must be cold before you ton it up.

To make a cake the way of the royal princes, the lady Elizabeth, daughter to king Charles the first

Take halfe a peck of flower, halfe a pinte of rose water, a pint of ale, yeast, a pint of cream, boil it, a ound and a halfe of butter, six eggs, leaf out the white, four pound of Currans, one half pound of sugar,

7   The same laid to the belly of a woman provoketh the tearms and maketh apt for conception.

Sir Edward Terril's salve
Called the chief of all salves

Take rosin, eight ounces, virgiens wax and frankincence of each fore ounces, mastick one ounce, harts suet four ounces, camphires two drams, beat the rosin, mastick and frankincense in a morter together to a fine pouder, then melt the resin and wax together, then put in the pouders and when the[y] are all well melted, strain it through a Cloath into a pottle of white wine and boil it together, till it be somewhat thick then let it Cool, and put in the Camphire and four ounces of venice turpentine drop by drop, lest it clumper, stiring it continually, then make it up into rolls and do with it to the pleasure of god and the health of man.

The vertues and use of it

1   It is good for all wounds and sores old or new in any place.
2   It clenseth all festers in the flesh and heals more in nine dayes, then other salves cure in a moneth.
3   It suffers no dead flesh to ingender or abide where it Comes.
4   It cureth the head-ach, rubbing the temples therewith.
5   It cuereth a saltfleam fall.
6   It healeth sinews that grow stiff, or spring with labour, or wax dry for want of blood.
7   It draweth out rusty iron, arrow heads, stubs, splints, thorns, or whatsoever is fixed in the flesh or wound.
8   It cureth the biting of a mad dog or pricking of any venemous creature.
9   It cureth all felons or white flaws.
10   It is good for all festering cankers.
11   It helpeth all aches of the liver spleen, kidneys, back, sides, arms or legs.

To make a dead plaister

Take two pound and fore ounces of the best and greenest sallet oyl: with a pound good red lead* and a pound of white lead.* Beat them well into dust, then take twelve ounces of Castle sope, incorporate all thees well together in a well glassed and great earthen pot that the sope may com upwards: set it on a small fire of Coales the space of one our and a halfe, allwaes stirring it with an iron ball or round pommil; them mak your fire somwhat bigger: until it be the colour of oyl, then drop a little on the board: and if it cleave neither to your finger nor the board: then it is enough. Then take the Clothes and make them into what breadth or size you please in Sear Cloth. Let not your Cloth be coarse, but of a reasonable vening holland; and when you have dipped them, then rub them with a stick or stone. It will last two years and the

elder the better. As long as it will stick it is good.

The vertues of the leaden plater

1 If it be lade to the Stomack it provoketh appitite: and taketh away any grief in the same.

2 If lade to the belly it is a present remedy for the ache

3 If lade to the reines of the back, it cureth and healeth the bloudy flux, the runing of the reans, heat in the liver or weakness in the back.

4 It healeth all bruises and swelling it taketh away aches, it breake the felons, pushes, and other impostumes, and healeth them.

5 It draweth out any running humer without breaking the Skin and being applied to the fundament it healeth any disease there growing.

6 The same laid to the head is good for the eyes.

The Lead referred to is a toxic substance and should not be used.

V

For a stich

Take Camomial: and make it dri between 2 dishes on a Chaffing dish of Coals and so bind it to the place.

For one that is poisoned

Take green rue: wash it and temper it with whit wine: and give it to him to drink.

For worms: boils: and botches

Take roasmari: and eat it fasting: with bread and honey: and you shall have no worms, boils or botches.

To make one sleep

Take lettuce and pound them and wring out the Juice and drink it.

For the wormes

Take worm wood, rue, small leeke, of each a handful, dry them in a pan till the[y] are hot then have ready your litell thin bag as broad as a trencher and bind them

to her stomake at night hot and let them ly all night. So do for three nights to gather haveing fresh every night.

[Another recipe for the worms]

Give her every morning a drought of posit drink wherein hath bin boyled half a handful of sage and roosmary every night: when she gooeth to bed give her a drought of milke or posit drink wherein hath bin boyled fore cloves of garlick pilled and cut.

To make sawces for roast Chickens

1   Gravy: and the Juice or slices of orange.
2   Butter: verjuice: and gravy of the Chicken: or mutten gravy
3   Butter and vinegar boyled together. Put to it a little sugar: then make thin sops of bread: lay the roast Chickens on them and serve them up hot.
4   Take sorrel: wash and stamp it: then have thin slices of manchent: put them in a dish with som vinegar: straed sorrel: sugar: some gra[v]y: beaten Cinnamon: beaten butter and som slices of orange or limon: and strew thereon som cinnamon and sugar.
5   Take sliced oranges and put to them a little white wine, rose water: beaten mace: ginger: some sugar and butter: and set them on a Chaffing dish of coales and stew them: then have som slices of manchet on the dish finely carved: and lay the Chickens being roasted on the sawce.

To make an excellaent surfeit water

Take Celendine: rosemary: rue pellitory of spain: scabious: angelica: pimpernel: worm wood: mugwort: bettoni: agrimoni: balm: dragon and tormetil: of each half a pound: sread [shred] them very small: and put them into a narrow mouthed pot: and put to them 5 quarts of whit wine: stop it Clos and let it stand 3 das and nits stirring it morning and evening then tak the hearbs from the wine and distil them in an ordinary stil: and when you have distilled the hearbs: distil the wine also: wherein is Virtue for a weak stomack: take 3 or 4 spoonfuls at any time.

For deafness

Take wild mint: mortifie it and squees it in the hand till it render Juice: then take it with its Juice and put it into the ear. Chang it oftt: this will help the deafness if the person ever heard before.

For the Cough or stopping of the breath

Take syrup of hore hound: hysop: liquorish: of each an ounce and take there of every morning a spoonful or two.

To make sawces for roast pidgeons

1 Gravy and Juice of orange.

2 Boyled parsli minced: and put amongst som butter: and beaten up thick.

3 Gravy: Clarret wine and an onion stued together with a littel salt.

4 Vine leaves Roasted with the pidgens minced: and put in Claret wine and salt boyled together: som butter and gravy.

5 Sweet butter and Juice of orang: beat together and made thick.

6 Miced onians boyled in Claret wine almost dry: then put to it nutmeg sugar: gravy of the fowl: and a littel pepper.

To make sawce for duck or mallard

1 Onions sliced: and Carrets cut up squar lik dice: boyled in whit wine: strong broth: som gravy: minced parsly: savory Chopped: mace and butter: being stewed together it will serve for divers wild fowll: but most proper for water fowll.

2 Vinegar and sugar boyled to a syrup with too or three Cloves and Cinnamon: or Cloves onely.

3 Oystr liquor: gravy of the fowl: whole onions byled in it, notmegs and an Anchovy: if the fowls be lean fars and lard them.

To make green sawce for pork, Chickens, lam or Kid

Stamp sorrel with whit bread and pared pippens in a stone or wooden mortar: put sugar to it and wine vinegar: then stran it thorow a fine Cloth pretty thick. Dish it into sawces and scrap sugar on it.

To make saces for a stubbl gooce

1 Take sowre apples: slice them and boyle them in beer all to mash: then put to them sugar and beaten butter: sometimes for variety add barberries: and the gravy of the fowl.

2 Roast sowre apples or pippins: strain them and put to them vinegar: sugar: gravy: barberries: grated bread: beaten Cinnamon: mustard and boyled onions strained and put to it.

6   Chopped parsley, Verjuice, butter: sugar and gravi boyled together.
7   Take Vinegar: butter: and Currans put them in a pipkin with sweet hearbs finely minced: the yolkes of hard eggs: and 2 or 3 slices of the brownest of the leg: mince it also: some Cinnamon: ginger: sugar and salt.
8   Pickled Capers and gravy: or gravy and samphire: Cut a inch long.
9   Chopped parsly and vinegar.
10   Salt: pepper: and Juice of oranges.
11   Stewed prunes: wine: and sugar.
12   Whit wine: gravy: large mace and bitter [?butter] thickened with two or three yolks of Eggs.
13   Oysters liquor and gravy boyled together: with eggs and Verjuice to thicken it: then Juice of oranges and slices of lemons over all.
14   Onions chopped with sweet hearbs, vinegar and salt boyled together.

To make several Sawces for roast veal
1   Juice of orange: gravy: nutmeg: and sliced limon on it
2   Gravy: Claret: nutmeg: vinegar: butter: sugar: and oranges melted together.
3   Vinegar and butter.
4   All manner of sweet hearbs Chopped small with the yoalks of 2 or 3 eggs: boyl them in vinegar: butter: and a few bread crumbs:

Currans: beaten Cawnam sugar: and a whole Clove or two put in under the veal: with Clices of orange and lemon about the dish.
5   Claret: sawce of boyled Carrats and boyled quinces: stamped and straned with limon: nutmeg: pepper: rose vinegar sugar and verjuice boyled to an indifferent height or thickness: with a few whole Cloves.

To make Sawces for rost pork
1   Gravy: Chopted sage: and onions boyled togeter with som pepper.
2   Mustard and vinegar and pepper.
3   Apples pared: quartred: and boyled in fare water: with som sugar and butter.
4   Gravi: onians: vinegar: pepper.

To make sawces for rabbets
1   Beat butter: and rub the dish with a Clove of garlick or shelot.
2   Sage and parsly minced: rowl it in a ball with som butter: and fill the belly with this stuffing.
3   Beaten butter with limon and pepper.
4   In french fashion: onions minced small and fried: and mingled with mustard and pepper.
5   The rabbet being roasted, wash the belly with the gravy of mutton: and add to it a slice or two of lemon.

To smooth the skin and take away morphew and freckles
Anoint your face with the bloud of a hare or a bull: and this will take away morphew and freckles and smooth the skin.

To pickle Cucumbers
Wash your cucumbrs clean: and dry them with a cloth: then take som water: vinegar: salt: fennel tops and some dill tops and a little mace: make it salt enough and sharp enough to the tast: then boyle it a while and then take it of and let it stand till it be Cold then put in the cucumbrs: and lay a board on the top to keep them down: and tye them up close: and within a week they will be fit to eat.

To pickel red and whit Currans
Take vinegar and white wine with so much sugar as will make it sweet: then take your red and white Corrans before not fully ripe and give them one rinse warm: so cover them over in the same pickle: keeping them all was under liqure.

To pickle flowers of all sorts
Put them into a gallipot or glass with as much sugar as the(y) weigh: fill them up with wine vinegar: to a pint of vinegar a pound of sugar and a pound of flowers: so keep them for sallads and boyled meats.

To make sawces for green Gees
Take the Juice of sorrel mixed with calded gooseberries and served on sippets with sugar and beaten butter.

To make sawce for land fowll
Take byled prunes and stran them with the blood of the fowl: cinnamon: gingar and sugar: boyle it to an indiffernt thickness and serve it in sawcers: and serve in the dish with the fowl: gravy and sawce of the same fowl.

To make divers sawces for roast mutton
1   Take gravi capers: samphire: and salt and steu them well together.
2   Watr: onions: claret wine: sliced nutmeg: and gravi boyled up.
3   Whole onions stewed in strong broth or gravy: white wine: pepper: pickled capers: mace: and 3 or 4 slices of a lemon.
4   Mince a little roast mutton hot from the spit: and add to it some chopped parsley and onions: Veriuice or Vinegar: ginger: and pepper: stew it very tender in a pipkin and serve it under any Joynt with some gravy of the mutton.
5   Onions: claret liquar: capers: claret gravy: nutmeg: and salt boyled together

To get the steins of
fruits out of any linen c[l]oth

Take them before they are washed: and
with a little butter rub every spot
well: then let the cloth lie in scalding
hot milk awhile and when it
is a little cooler: rub the spotted p[l]aces in
the milk till you see they are quite out,
and then wash it with water and soap.

To tak out any greasie spots
out of silk stuff or Cloth

Take a linen Clo Rag and wet it very well
in fare water: then with a pare of tongs
put a live sea coale or wood coal upon
the rag: and hastily Close the rest of the rag
about the cole: and presently lay it upon
the greasie spot whilst it is smoking hot:
and when you perceive it to cool do so
again: and so do till you find the spots are
quite taken out.

How to make clean plate

Wash your plate first in soap suds and dry
it: then if there be any spots rub them
out with salt and Vinegar: then anoint
your plat all over with Vinegar and
Chalk: then lay it in the son [sun] or before the fire
to dry: then rub it of with warm
linen Cloths very well and it will
look like new.

To [?clean] the [?silver]

There is no beter thing to wash the [?silver] with:
to keep it smoot and to scower it clean
than to wash it every [?month] with brandy:
wherein you have steeped a little flower
of brimstone: and the next day wip it
only with a Cloth.

To mak a salve for the lips

Take two ounces of whit bees wax: and
slice it thin: then melt it over the fire
with two ounces of sallet oyl: and a little whit
sugar Candi: and when you see it is well
incorporated take it of the fire and let it stand
till it be cold: then set the skillet on the fire
agane: till the bottom is warm and so turn it
out: anoint your lips or sore nose
or sore nipples with this: and it will heal
them.

To keep the teeth Clean and sound

Take Common white salt one ounce: as
much Cuttle bone: beat them together and
rub your teeth with them every morning
and then wash them with fair water.

To [?keep] the hands [white] and [?] like

Take daffadil in clean water till it
grow thick: then put thereto powder of
Cantarium and stir them together: put
thereto two eggs and stir them well
together: and with this ointment anint your
hands: and within 3 or 4 days of use thereof
they will be white: clear and soft.

outwards: and when they are near dri
pluck them out with your hands and smooth
them with an iron on the wrong side.

To make Clean points and laces

Take whit bread of half a day old: and
cut it in the middle: and pare the crust from the
edge so that you may not hurt yur
points when you rub them: then lay them
upon a table on a Clean Cloth: and rub
them very well with the whit bread all
over: then take a clean small brish and rub
over the bread very well: till you think
you have rubbed it very clean then
take your point or lace and shak the bread
clean of: then tak a clean linen cloth and
gentli slap it over often times: thus
you may get the soyl of from white satten
tafaty tabby: or any coloured silk: provided
it be not greasie or too much soiled.

Direction to wash and starch points

Take your points and put them into a tent:
then make a strong ladder with the best
soap you can get: then dip a brush
in that ladder: and sound and rub your points
on both sids: so do till you have
washed it in your laddars: then wash it in
fair water alone: then wash it in blew water: and when you have so
done
take starch made thin with water

and with your brush on the wrong
side wash it over with it: so let
it dry: then lay your points upon a
table and with an ivory bodkin made
for the purpose: run into every close
and narrow part of it to open it betwixt
the gimp or over cast likewise into
every ilet hole to open them.
For the laces: likewise you have pulled them
out well with your hands: you must
iron them on the wrong side: let the water
be warm wherewith you mak your
ladder when you take them out of the
tent. Iron them on the wrong side:
let not the water be too blew with
which you wash them.

To make clean gold and silver lace

Take the lase of from your garment: and lay
it upon a table: and with a brush rub
it over very well with burnt allum
beaten fine: till you find it to be
of the right colour: then shak it very well
and wip it very well wit a clean linen
cloth oftentimes over.

To get spots of ink out of linen cloth

Before that you suffer it to be washed: lay it all
night in Urien [urine]: the next day rub all the
spots in Urien as if you were washing in
water: then lay it in Urien another
night: and then rub it agan: and so do till
you find they be quit out.

Thus you may starch lawns
but observe to iron them on the
wrong sid: and upon a Cloth wetted
and wrung out agan: sometime if you
pleas instead of stach you ma[y] la[y] gum
araback in water: and when it is
dissolved wet the lawns in that
instid of starch: and hold them to the
fir as before directed: clapping them
and rubbing them till the are very
clear.

Directions for washing white and black sarsenets

Let them be veri smooth and sthreight upon
a board: and if there be any dirty places
soap them a litl: then take a small hard
brush and sop it wel: then dip the brush in
water: and with it make a pritti thick ladder:
then take the brush and rub your sarsenet
wel the right way of the sarsnet: sideways
of the brush: and when you have washed one side
well: tirn it and wash the other: then have a
clen ladder scalding hot and cast your hoods
in double into it and cour [cover] it and stil as fast
as you wash them cast tem into it: you
must give them 3 like washes upon the board:
and like the first ladder let the other be veri
hot: and cast them in and scald everi time:
then make up a scalding hot ladder
into which put some gom arabick steeped
before in water: and some small thin blew, a

little: let them be doubled up in that close
coured [covered] for one hour: when you come for to
take them out be sure you dip them all
very well all over: and then fold them up
to a very small size: and squeeze them smooth
betwext your hands: then smoak them
over brimstone: then draw them between
your hands every way till they be small,
certain half dry: then smooth them with the
hot Irons the same way you did wash
them and upon the right side of the sarsenet.

To wash Coloured silk

They are done the same way with the white:
only ther must be no blew nor smoking
over brimstone.

To wash black sarsenets

The[y] are washed the same way with the other:
only rinse in strong beer cold without
any gum: and iron upon the wrong side and
on a woollen Cloth.

To wash silk stockings

Mak a strong ladder with soap: and little
pretti hot: then lay your stockings on a table:
and take a piece of such Cloth: as the seamen
use for ther sails: doublit up and
rub them soundli with it: turn them first
on one sid and then on the other: til they have passed
through 3 ladders: then rinse them well
and hang them to dry with the wrong side

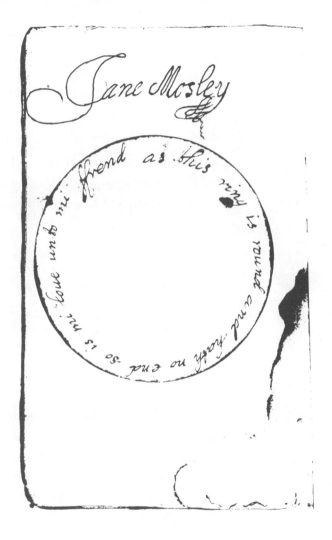

Directions for starching of tiffany

Sop [soap] not the tiffany save only on the
hems or laces with Crown soap: the[n]
wash them very wel in three ladders
preti hot: and let your last ladder
be mad thin of the soap: do not
rinse them nor wring them hard: then
dry them over brimiton and keep them
all the tim from the air for that will
spoil them: then make your starch
of a reasonable thicknes: and
blew it according to your liking and
to a quarter of a pound of starch
put as much allum as an haslenot:
boyl it very wel and stran it:
and whil it is hot wet your tiffanies
with it very well: and lay
them in a Cloth to keep them from
drying: then with your hands clean
and dry them: then hold your tiffanies
to a good fire(e) til the[y] be thorow
hot: then clap them and rub them
between your hands from the fire
till you see the be very clear: then
shap[e] them by a piece of paper: cut
out bi them before the[y] were washed:
and iron them with a good hot iron
and the will look glossy lik new tiffanies.

put in 10 eggs yolks and whites, 5 spoonfuls of english honey and as much wheat flower as will make all this as thick as a salve, and so stir it very well together, and put it close up in a pot that it take no air, and so keep it for your use.

A bag to smell unto for melancholy or to cause one to sleep

Take dry rose leaves, keep them close in a glass which will keep them sweet, then take powder of mints, powder of Cloves in a gross powder, and put the same to the rose leaves, then put all these together in a bag; and take that to bed with you, and it will cause you to sleep, and it is good to smell unto at other times.

For the spitting of Blood

Take the juice of bettony tempered with goats milk, and drink thereof three or foure mornings together.

An ointment for all sores, cuts, swellings, and heat

Take a good quantity of smallage, and mallows, and put thereto 2 pounds of bores grease, 1 pound of butter, and oil of neats foot a quantity, stamp them well together, then fry them and strain them into an earthen pot and keep it for your use.

For boils or kibes, or to draw a sore

Take strong ale and boyl it from a pint to four spoonfuls, and so keep it, it will be an ointment.

To make cammomil oyl

Shred a pound of cammimil, and knead it into a pound of sweet butter, melt it, and strain it.

For the falling sickness

Take the roots of single pionie, grate them, drink them, and wear some of them about your neck.

For a scald-head

Take a handful of grovers shreds and a handful of dock roots, the pith taken out, and boil them in strong ale until they be reasonable thick, and annoint the head therewith.

For the Itch

Take a pound of butter, unwashed and unsalted, 3 good handfuls of red sage, and as much brimstone beaten into powder, as a walnut, boil these well together, and strain it, and put in half an ounce of ginger beaten small.

An excellent receipt against a Cough of a Consumption

Take a quarter of a pound of the best honey, a quarter of a pint of Conduit water, boil them as long as any white scum ariseth, and take it off, then take a quarter of a pound of the best blew currans, put them on the fire in a pint of fare water; boil them until they be tender, then pour the water from them, and bruise them through a hair sive and put that 'juice', and honey together, add to it one ounce of the powder of liquorice, one ounce of the powder of annise seeds; mix all these together and put them in a gally pot, and when it is cold tye it up; the party troubled may take of it upon the point of a knife morning or evening, as often as the coughs taketh them.

For the wind Colick

Take the flowers of walnuts and dry them to powder, and take of them in your ale or beer, or in your broth as you like best, and it will help you.

For the Canker in the mouth or nose

Take the ashes of green leaves of holly, with half so much of the burnt powder of allum: blow with a quil into the place grieved, and it will help man, child, or beast.

A medicine for the worms

Take one penniworth of alloes with the like quantity of ox gall and mithridate, mix them together, and lay them on the childs navel upon a plaister.

A green salve for an old sore

Take a handful of groundsel, as much hous leek, of marigold leaves a handful, pick and wipe these herbs clean, but wash them not, then beat all these herbs in a wooden bowl as small as is possible then strain out all the juice and put in a quantity of hogs grease, as much as 2 eggs, beat all these together again, then put in the juice again, and

be well incorporated together use
it to eat morning, noon, and night.

A medicine for the worms
Take one peniworth of alloes with the
like quantity of ox gall and mithridate,
mix them together and lay them on the
Childs navel upon a plaister.

Against the wind
Take Cummin seed, steep them in sack
24 hours, dry them by the fire, and
hull them, then take fennell seeds,
Carraway seed and annise seed, beat
all these together, and take every
morning half a spoonful in broth or better
Another
for fasting.
Take enula Compana, grate it, and
drink half a spoonful, fasting.

For the biting of a dog
Take ragworth, chop it, and boil it with
unwasht butter to an ointment

For to Cleanse the head
Take pellitory of spain, and chew the roots
three dayes, a good quantity, and it will purge
the head, and away the ach, and fasten the
teeth in the gums.

For an Ich or any scurf of the body
Take elecampane rots [roots] or leaves, stamp
them; and fry them with fresh grease,
straine it into a dish, and annoint
the patient.

For one that is bruised with a fall
Take horse dung, and sheeps suet,
boil them together, and apply it to the
same place, being laid upon a cloth.

A syrrup for the pain in the stomach
Take 2 good handfuls of young rue,
boil it in a quart of good white
wine vinegar till it be half consumed,
so soon as it is through cold, strain it,
and put to every pint of the liquor
a pound and a quarter of loaf
sugar, and boil it till it Come to a
syrrup, when you use it, take a good
spoonful of this in the morning fasting
and eat nor drink nothing for 2 or 3
hours after, it is good for pain in the
stomach that process of windy vapour,
and is excellent good for the lungs
and obstructions of the breast.

J

redness be turned into a grave
Colour, but you must not leave
stirrin it till the matter be turned
into a perfect black Colour, or as
pitch, then drop a little upon a
wooden trencher, and if it
cleave not to the trencher, nor
your finger, it is enough.
Then take the long linnen clothes,
and dip them therein and
make your searcloth thereof: the(y)
will keep twenty years: let your
powder of your lead be searsed
very fine, and shred the
soap small.

The Vertues of this searcloth are:-

being laid to the stomack, it doth
provock appetite, and taketh
away any pain in the stomack;
being laid to the belly it is a
present remedy for the Cholick;
being laid to the back, it is a present
remedy for the flux and running
of the reins, heat of the kidnies,
and weakness of the back; it
helpeth all swellings and bruises,
taketh away aches. It breaketh
fellons and other imposthumes,
and healeth them, it draweth
out any running humour
and helpeth them without breaking
of the skin, and being applied
to the fundaments helpeth any
disease there; it helpeth all ould
sores and will be made in six [h]ours.

For worms in children
Wormseed boiled in beer or ale,
and then sweeten it with
clarified honey, and let them
drink it.

**A very good Conserve for the help
of a Consumption and Cough**
Tak half a pound of blew raisins,
the blackest sort is the best, and
stone them, and skin them, and two
ounces of whit sugar candy, and two
ounces of oyl of sweet almonds and
bruise them well, and when they

I

20 It is a grate preserver of health, and means of long life taken sometimes in mede.

21 It may be used as a treacle or bezar against surfeits.

22 It is a general good upon all occasions and may given at all times when you do not know what the disease is, in any of the aforesaid liquors.

The dose for a man or woman is from one scruple to two scruple, and to a boy or girl twelve or fourteen grains in Convenient liquors.

A most sertin and proved medicine agains all manner of pestilence and plague, be it never so vhement

Take an onion, and cut it overthwart, then make a little hole in either piece, the which you shall fill with fine treacle and set the peces together as they were before: after this wrap them in a fine wet linnen cloth putting it to roast, and covered in the embers or ashes, and when it is roasted enough press out all the juice of it, and give the patient a spoonful, and immediately he shall feel himself better, and shall without fail be healed.

A rare searcloth with the vertues

Take of oyl olive one pound and a halfe, red lead* one pund and a halfe, of white lead* one pund, Castle-soap 4 ounces. Put your oil olive in a pipkin and put thereto your oil of baies and your Castle soap: seeth these over a gentle fire, and melted together, then strew a little red lead and white, being mingled in powder, still stirring it with a spatler of wood and so strew in more of your lead by little an little till all be in, stiring it still by the bottom to keep it from burning, for an hour and halfe together, then make the fire some what bigger, till their

The lead referred to is a toxic substance and should not be used

H

The virtue of a root called Contra Yerua being made into a fine powder

1   It withstands the plague being taken in treacle water.

2   It is good in all pestilent diseases, taken in posset drink with saffron.

3   It is good against a fever taken [in] cardus water.

4   It is a great antidote against all poysons taken in sallet oil.

5   It doth cure the biting of a mad dog, drunk in rose vinegar and then drink nothing else but spring water during the cure.

6   It causeth a speedy delivery given in balm water, bettony water, or in burnt wine.

7   It doth take away the after throws given in the same liquors.

8   It is a good Cordial in all fits of the mother given in rue water.

9   It is very soveraign in soouning fits, given in sack or borrage water.

10   It is very powerful to withstand all melancholy, given in sack.

11   It doth help convulsions in Children given in spring water.

12   It helpeth the worms given in goats milk.

13   It is good for a short breath given in rue water.

14   It helpeth the head pain given in rue water or rosemary water.

15   It helpeth the yellow jaundies given in celendine water.

16   It is very powerful in the palsie given in sage water.

17   It is a good antidote against the gout given in sage water.

18   It withstandeth the growing of the stone in the reins given in rhenish wine

19   It causeth a good and quiet sleep taken in white wine.

on the fire, again a little while
and drink of it morning and evening.

To take away hoarsness

Take a turnip, cut a hole in the top
of it, and fill it up with brown
sugar candy, and so roast it in
the embers, and eat it with butter.

To take away the head ach

Take the best sallet oyl, and the
glass half full with tops of poppy
flowers which grow in the corn,
set this in the sun a fortnight,
and so keep it all the year, and
anoint the temples of your
head with it.

For a Cough

Take sallet oyl, aqua vite, and
sack, of each an equal quantity,
beat them all together, and before
the fire rub the soles of your
feet with it.

Plantaine

A perfect water for the sight

Take sage, fennel, vervain,
bettony, eyebright, pimpernel,
Cinquefoil, and heabgrace, lay
all these in white wine one night.
Still it in a stillatory of glass.
This water did restore the
sight of one that was blind 3 years
before.

A plaister to heal any sore

Take of sage, herb grace, of each like
quantity, ribwort, plantain and dasie
roots, more than half so much of
each of them with wax, fresh
grease, and rosin make it a salve,
if the flesh grow proud then put
always upon the plaister, before
you lay it to the sore, burnt allum,
and it will Correct the flesh.

A Salve to heal all manner of sores and Cuts

Take one pint of turpentine, one pint of oil of olives, a quarter of a pinte of running water, nine branches of rosemary, 1 ounce of unwrought wax, 2 ounce roses, seeth all these together in a little pan over the fire, let it seeth untill there arise a little white scum upon it, then stir it untill one quarter be consumed. Then take of from the fire, strain it through a coarse cloth but it must be done quickly after it be taken from the fire for cooling, after you have strained it in an earthen pot let it cool, and keep it for your use.

To make oil of sage good for the grief in any joint or for any ack

Take sage and parsley, seeth them all in oil olive till it be thick and greene.

A mediciene to purge and amend the heart, stomach, spleen, liver, lungs and brain

Take alexander, water cresses, young mallowes, borrage and fennel roots pared, mercury,* harts tongue, and clare, and make of these pottage.

To drive infections diseases from the heart

Take mithridate and Centory, of each 2 ounces, 8 spoonfuls of dragon water, one pint of white wine, 7 spoonfuls of aqua vite, boil al together a little, strain it, then set it

E   * *Mercury refers to the pot herb Allgood*

To heal a prick with a nail or thorn

Take too handfuls of celendine, as much
orpen, cut it small, and boile it with
oile olive and unwrought wax,
then strain it and use it.

To stop the bleeding of a cut or wound

Take hop, stamp it, and put it into the wound, if
hop will not do it then put
to it vinegar with the hop.

Doctor Willoughbies water

Take galingal, cloves, cubebs, ginger,
mellilot, cardamome, mace,
nutmegs, of each a dram, and of the
Juice of celendine halfe a pint and
mingle all thes made in powder with
the said juice, and with a pint of good
aqua vite and three pints of good
white wine, and put all these together
in a still of glass, and let it stand
all night, and on the morrow still it
with an easie fire as maybe.

The vertue is of secret nature. It
dissolveth the swelling of the lungs
without any grievance, and the
same lungs being wounded or perished
it helpeth and comforteth, and
it suffereth not the blood to putryfie.
He shall never need to be let blood
that useth this water, and it suffers
not the heart to be burnt, nor
melancholy or flegm to have
domenion above nature, it also
expelleth the rheum, and purifieth
the stomach. It preserveth the uisage
or memory, and destroyeth the
palsie, and if this water be given
man or woman labouring towards
death, one spoonfull relieveth. In the
summer time use once a week fasting
the quantity of a spoonfull, and
in winter two spoonfulls.

to powder, sal gemme 12 penny weight, the flowers of pomegranates, white coral, of each a six penny weight, make all these into powdor, and with a little rosewater, and a sage leaf rub the teeth.

For sun-burn

Take the juice of a Lemmon and a little bay salt, and wash your hands with it, and let them dry of themselves, wash them again and you shall find aull the sobs and stains gone.

For the tooth ach

Take pepper and grains, of each one ounce, bruise them, and compound them with the water of the diseased and lay it outward on the cheek against the place greaved, and it will help it for ever after.
Another

Take dried sage, make powder of it, burnt allum, bay salt, make all in fine powder, and lay it to the tooth where the pin is and also rub the gums with it.

A powder against the wind in the stomach

Take ginger, cinnamon, and gallingal, of each 2 ounces, aronise seed, carraway and fennel, seeds of each 1 ounce, long pepper, grains, mace and nutmegs, of each half an ounce, setwel half a dram, make all in powder, and put thereto 1 pound of white sugar, and use this after your meat, or before at your pleasure; at all times it comforteth the stomach marvellously, carrieth away wind and causeth a good digestion.

C

For the tooth ach

Take spearmints and ground ivy, of each a hanful, and a good spoonful of bay salt, stamp all these very well togeter, and boil tem in a pint of the strongest vinegar that you can get, let these boyle all together until they come to a quarter of a piant, then strain it and put it into a glas and stop it very close, when your teeth do ake take a spoonful of it blood warm, and hold it in your mouth on that side the pain is.

To make the teeth standfast

Take roots of vervain in cold wine, and wash the teeth therewith.

A powder to keep the teeth clean, and from being worm eate.

Take rosemary burned to ashes, cuttles bone, harts horn burned

Bi Jane Mosley (upside down)

The Spanish Ladies Love to an english gentleman

will you hear a spanish Lady
how she wooed an english man
garments gay as rich as may be
deckt with Jewels had she on
of a comely countenance
and grace was she
and by birth and parentage
of a high degree
as his prisoner there he kept her
in his hands her life did lye
Cupids hands did tye her faster
by the liking of her eye
in his courteous company
was all her Joy
to favour him in anything
she was not coy
at last there came commandment
fo(r) to set the Ladies free
with their Jewels still adorned
none to do them injury
alas then said the Lady gay
full woe is me
O let me still sustain this kind captivity
Gallant captain shew some pity
to a Lady in distress
Leave me not within the city
for to dye in heaviness
thou has set this present day my body free
but my heart in prison strong
remains with thee

A

(vi)

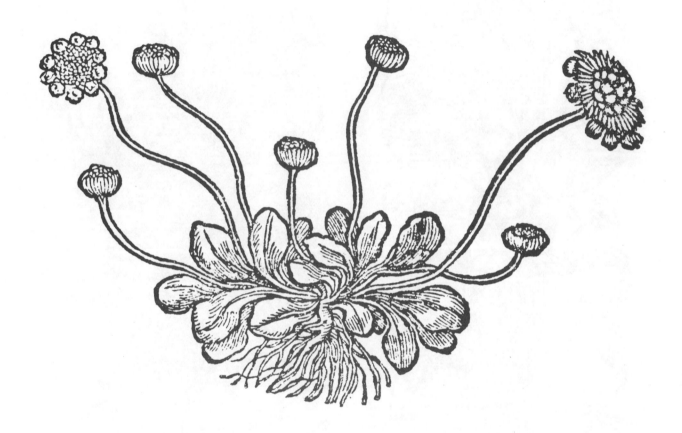

(v)

warm milk, curdled with ale, wine, or other liquor, often with sugar and spices

Posnet
a small metal pot for boiling with a handle and three feet

Pottage
a dish of vegetables, or vegetables and meat, boiled with water until soft; or a thick soup

Powder Cantuarium
? powder made from Canterbury bells

Proud Flesh
overgrown flesh in a healing wound, caused by excessive granulation round the edges of the wound

Purslaine
purslaine, a low succulent herb used in salads, or as a pot herb, or for pickling

Purttenance
purtenance, the edible inward parts of an animal

Push
pimple, pustule, or boil

Ragwort
several species of the plant family **Senecio**

Reins
the kidneys; here also used for the urinary system generally

Rheum
a watery, mucous discharge caused by cold

Ribwort
the narrow leaved plantain

Rine
rind

Rocket
an annual plant with purple veined white flowers and acrid leaves used for salads; yellow rocket is winter cress

Rosin
resin

Rowle
roll

Rue
an evergreen shrub with bitter, strong scented leaves

Sack
a class of white wines formerly imported from Spain and the Canary Islands

Saffron
the dried orange red stigmas of the saffron plant

Sallet
salad

Sal gemme
rock salt

Salt fleam
salt fleum, watering eyes; salt fleam fall or streaming eyes

Salve
a healing ointment

Samphire
a seaside plant with fleshy, aromatic, salty leaves

Sarsenet
a very fine, soft silk material

Sawce
sauce

Scald head
a head infected by ring worm, or in the late 17th century other scalp infections

Scruple
an apothecary's unit of weight equalling 20 grains or 1/24 oz

Scum
skim

Seall
sealwort or Solomon's seal

Searcloth
cerecloth, cloth smeared

with wax or some glutinous substance used as a winding sheet, or a plaster

Searse
searce, to sieve through a bristle sieve

Seffron
saffron

Senee
senna, the dried leaves or pods of a cassia shrub

Shelot
shallot

Shog
shake

Sinamon
cinnamon

Sippet
a small piece of toasted or fried bread usually served in soup or with meat or for dipping into gravy

Skum
skim

Smallage
strictly wild celery, but more loosely plants of the celery and parsley family especially water parsley

Soouning
swooning

Son
sun

Sorrel
a group of small perennial plants with a sour taste

Spatler
spatula

Spearmint
common garden mint

Spigot
see forset

Spinnage
spinach

Sporragus
asparagus

Spring with labour
sprain

Stamp
pound

Stillatory
a still

Stockfish
cod and fish of the same family cured without salt, split open and dried hard in the air

Suckery
succory or wild chicory

Surfeit
sickness arising from overeating or over drinking

Suttory
? succory

Tabby
silk taffeta

Tafaty
taffeta

Tansey
tansy, a herbaceous plant with yellow flowers, an aromatic scent and bitter taste

Tent
? a protective covering. The word can mean a portable shelter, a roll of soft, absorbent material for searching and cleaning a wound, or an embroidery frame

Thyme
an aromatic pot herb

Tiffany
a thin transparent silk, or a transparent gauze muslin, or cobweb lawn, much used for head dresses and sieves

Time
thyme

Tormetil
a low growing herbaceous plant with astringent roots

Treacle
a kind of salve used as an antidote against venomous bites, poisons and malignant diseases; also treacle in the modern sense

Trencher
a flat piece of wood on which meat was served and carved, a plate

Trug
a wooden milk pan, or a shallow oblong basket made of wood strips

Turmeric
powder made from an aromatic pungent root of an Indian plant

Umbles
the edible inward parts of an animal, usually a deer

Unwrought wax
? wax straight from the beehive

Urien
urine

Venice turpentine
a variety of turpentine

Verjuice
acid juice of green or unripe grapes, crab-apples or other sour fruits, expressed and formed into a liquor

Vervain
a herbaceous plant of the verbena family, formerly much used in medicine

Virgiens wax
virgin wax, originally unworked wax, later a purified fine wax or white wax

Virginal
a keyed musical instrument, rather like a spinet but with no legs, common in England in the 17th century

Waa
water

Wormseed
various plants thought to be useful in worming

Wormwood
artemisia absinthium, a plant with a very bitter taste

Fennel
a fragrant umbelliferous plant with yellow flowers

Flegm
phlegm, mucus, or the coldness or dullness of character supposed to result from an excess of phelgm

Florentine
a kind of pie or tart, especially a meat pie

Flower
flour

Flux
an abnormally heavy flow of blood, excrement, urine etc from the bowels or bladder

Forset
faucet or tap

Frankincense
an aromatic gum resin

Frydayes pie
a pie suitable for Friday, a fast day on which Christians customarily abstained from eating flesh in commemoration of the Crucifixion of Jesus Christ

Fundament
buttocks and anus

Galingale
aromatic root of certain East Indian plants, or of **Cyperus longus,** an English species of sedge

Gall
a secretion of the liver, bile

Gallipot
a small, earthen, glazed pot

Genitors
genital organs

Gillyflower
clove scented flower, especially the clove scented pink

Gimp
silk, worsted or cotton twist with a cord running through it

Glassed
glazed

Grain
the smallest English unit of weight, 1/7000 of a pound avoirdupois, the common English pound of 16 ounces

Grains
grains of paradise, the capsules of **Amomum meleguetta**

Grave
colour
dull or sombre

Gravy
stock

Groundsel
any plant of the family **Senecio,** especially common groundsel

Groovers shreds
probably shreds or shavings of lead. Groover was a Derbyshire term for miner especially for the lead miner

Gum araback
gum arabic exuded by certain kinds of acacia

Grease
rendered animal fat

Hare
hair

Hartshorn
shaved or burned horn of harts, at this time the chief source of ammonia

Hartstongue
common name of **Scolopendrium vulgare**

Hearneshaw
heron

Herb grace
the plant, rue

Hipachrist bag
hippocras bag, a conical bag of cotton, linen or flannel, used as a filter

Horehound
a herb with white cottony down covering its stalk and leaves

Houseleek
the **Sempervivum** family of succulents, especially **Sempervivum tectorum**

Humer or humour
moisture, fluid or juice, natural or morbid

Hyssop
a small, bushy aromatic herb

Ilet
eyelet

Imposture
an abscess anywhere in the body

Jollap
jalop, a purgative drug

Kibe
a chapped or ulcerated chilblain

Kickshaw
a fancy dish, dainty but insubstantial, from the French **quelque chose**

Ladder
lather

Lawn
a fine linen

Lettice spinage
a variety of spinach

Mace
a spice, the dried outer covering of the nutmeg

Maden hare
one of the maiden hair ferns, **Adiantum capillus veneri,** once much used medicinally

Mallard
male wild duck

Mallow
a common wild plant with purply red flowers and hairy stems and leaves

Manchet
the finest kind of wheaten bread, or a roll or small loaf of this

Marmalet
marmalade

Marrow
fatty inner core of a bone, or the vegetable of the gourd family, depending on context

Mastic
a gum or resin exuded from the bark of certain trees

Mellilot
melilot, a leguminous plant, the dried flowers of which were much used for plasters and poultices

Mercury
the pot herb, Allgood

Mithridate
a powder regarded as an antidote against poisons and infectious diseases, here probably mustard

Morphew
a leprous or scurfy eruption

Motmeg
nutmeg

Mugwort
a plant **Artemisia vulgaris**

Musk
a substance secreted in a gland of the male musk deer, which is the basis of many perfumes, or a 17th century artificial preparation imitating it

Neat
an animal of the ox kind, an ox, bullock, cow or heifer

Orengado
the outer yellow rind of an orange

Orpen
orpine or orpin, a succulent herbaceous plant, one of the sedums, also called Live-long

Overthwart
across

Palsy
state of trembling or shaking

Peel
pall or cover, or a baker's shovel

Pennyweight
a small English unit of measure, weighing 20 to the ounce

Pill
peel

Pellitory of Spain
a plant from Barbary with a pungently flavoured root

Pimpernel
the plants Great Burnet and Salad Burnet

Pin
pain

Piony
peony

Pipkin
small earthenware or metal pot or pan

Pippin
numerous varieties of apple

Plaister
plaster

Point
a tagged lace or cord for fastening clothes or attaching hose to doublets

Pommil
pommel, a round knob

Ponado
panada, a dish made by boiling bread in water to a pulp and flavouring it

Porringer
a small basin from which soup, porridge or children's food was eaten

Posit
posset, a drink made of

Glossary

After throw
after birth

Agrimoni
agrimony, a family of plants, also used as the name of several unrelated plants

Alexander
horse parsley, an umbelliferous plant used for salads, with stalks tasting like celery

Alloes
aloes, a bitter purgative made from the condensed juices of the plants of the aloe family

Allum
alum, a mineral salt

Annise
anise, an umbelliferous plant, formerly confused with dill, the source of aniseed

Aqua vite
originally unrectified alcohol, here any form of spirits taken as a drink, probably brandy

Aronise
this reading is not clear. The word could be awnise, which is probably another version of anise

Balm
the herb, or yeast, or the froth from fermenting beer, depending on context

Barberry
or berberry, a shrub with spiny shoots and racemes of small yellow flowers which later form red, acid berries

Bettony
betony, a herb

Bezar
bezoar, a term for an antidote

Biles
boils

Blane
blain, blister, blotch or pustule

Bores grease
lard

Borrage
borage, a class of plants including the herb with blue flowers and prickly leaves and stems

Brimiton
brimstone, sulphur

Buck thorn
a maritime shrub with berries yielding a strong cathartic

Bugloss
a name for several plants in the borage class

Burdock
a coarse weedy plant with leaves like the dock, bearing burrs

Burrage
borage

**Cammimil
or camomial**
camomile, a herb

Camphire
camphor

Canker
an eating spreading sore or ulcer, a gangrene

**Cannam
or Cawnam sugar**
cane sugar. Sugar cane was bought as cane for

some dishes

Cardamom
a spice consisting of the seed capsules of certain E. Indian plants

Cardus water
juice or infusion of **cardus benedictus**, the Holy Thistle

Castle soap
Castile soap, a fine, hard soap made with olive oil and soda

Cawdle
caudle, a warm drink or a thin gruel mixed with ale or wine, sweetened and spiced

Celendine
celandine, a herb

Centory
Great centaury, a composite plant from which a botanical class has been named

Chafing dish
a portable grate or a utensil to hold burning fuel

Chalderon
chaldron or chawdron, entrails

Chewet
a dish of various kinds of meat and fish, minced and seasoned

Chine
backbone and adjoining flesh

Cimbals
sort of spongy-cake or doughnut

Cinammon
a spice, the inner bark of

an East Indian tree, brittle, fragrant and aromatic

Cinquefoil
the plant **Potentilla reptans**

Clare
clary, a pot herb

Clease
claws. Here the division of the calf's foot

Clumper
to form into lumps

Cod
seed pod

Coffin
pie dish, or a pastry case shaped like a pie dish

Coleflower
? cauliflower

Conduit water
water passed through pipes, which at this time would be made of lead

Coney
rabbit

Contra Yerua

Contra yerva, the counter herb or herb used as an antidote, also, as probably here, the rootstock of a tropical American plant used as a stimulant and tonic, and formerly as an antidote to snake bite

Coriander
an umbelliferous plant with aromatic seeds

Cubeb
berry of a climbing Javanese shrub, very like a grain of pepper, with a pungent spicy flavour

Cummin
an umbelliferous plant, with an aromatic seed

Curd
a coagulated substance made from milk by the action of acids

Cuttlesbone
internal shell of the cuttlefish

Dragon
dragon herb otherwise dragon wort, the common arum

Dragon water
the juices or an infusion of dragon wort

Drought
draught

Endiffe
endive

Elecampane
a plant with large yellow flowers and bitter aromatic leaves and roots

Enula campana
elecampane

Eringus
eryngo, the candied root of the sea holly

Eyebright
a small wild flower with about two dozen species, native to the British Isles, flower shaped like a hood

Farcing
stuffing with forcemeat, herbs and spices

Fall
flow, stream or effusion

Felon
small abscess or boil, an inflamed sore

Illustrations — "Leaves from Gerard's Herball"

Facsimile reproductions from the original

Pages A, M, Z

L	For boils or kibes, or to draw a sore	R	To make Sawces for rost pork
L	To make cammomil oyl	R	To make sawces for rabbets
L	For the falling sickness	S	To make sawces for roast pidgeons
L	For a scald-head	S	To make sawce for duck or mallard
M	Directions for starching of tiffany	S	To make green sawce for pork, Chickens, lam or Kid
N	Directions for washing white and black sarsenets	S	To make saces for a stubbl gooce
N	To wash Coloured silk	T	To make sawces for roast Chickens
N	To wash black sarsenets	T	To make an excelaent surfeit water
N	To wash silk stockings	T	For deafness
O	To make Clean points and laces	T	For the Cough or stopping of the breath
O	Direction to wash and starch points	U	For a stich
O	To make clean gold and silver lace	U	For one that is poisoned
O	To get spots of ink out of linen cloth	U	For worms: boils: and botches
P	To get the steins of fruits out of any linen c(l)oth	U	To make one sleep
P	To tak out any greasie spots out of silk stuff or Cloth	U	For the wormes
P	How to make clean plate	U	(Another recipe for the worms)
P	To (? clean) the (? silver)	V	To make a dead plaister
P	To mak a salve for the lips	V	The vertues of the leaden plater
P	To keep the teeth Clean and sound	W	Sir Edward Terril's salve Called the chief of all salves
P	To (? keep) the hands (white) and (?) like	X	Ar kings way to make mead
Q	To smooth the skin and take away morphew and freckles	X	To make a cake the way of the royal princes, the Lady Elizabeth, daughter to king Charles the first
Q	To pickle Cucumbers		
Q	To pickel red and whit Currans		
Q	To pickle flowers of all sorts		
Q	To make sawces for green Gees		
Q	To make sawce for land fowll		
Q	To make divers sawces for roast mutton		
R	To make several Sawces for roast veal		

Warning Great care should be taken in identifying the wild plants mentioned in the remedies. Umbelliferous hedge plants such as Alexanders and Hedge Parsley should not be confused with other members of that family, notably Water Dropwort and Hemlock, which are extremely poisonous. Cultivated Water Cress should always be used as the wild variety may be unsafe for consumption, and can be confused with its toxic relatives.

Contents

Jane Mosley's
REMEDIES

Designed and Published by Derbyshire Museum Service
1979

Jane Mosley